THE MIDDLE EAST

A NEW YORK TIMES BYLINE BOOK

W9-AGG-239

NEW YORK TIMES BYLINE BOOKS

THE
MIDDLE EAST

by Jay Walz

A NEW YORK TIMES BYLINE BOOK

ATHENEUM

NEW YORK

1969

TO AUDREY

who shared the experience of
this Middle East story

Copyright © 1965 by The New York Times Company
All rights reserved
Library of Congress catalog card number 65—27595
Published simultaneously in Canada by McClelland and Stewart Ltd.
Manufactured in the United States of America
Composition by H. Wolff, New York
Printed by The Murray Printing Company,
Forge Village, Massachusetts
Designed by Harry Ford
First Printing September 1965
Second Printing August 1966
Third Printing December 1966
Fourth Printing September 1967
Fifth Printing September 1969

CONTENTS

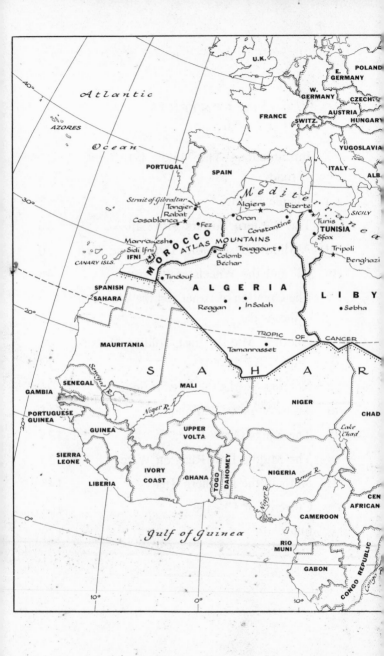

JAY WALZ

Jay Walz has been a foreign correspondent of *The New York Times* since 1958, when he took up a post in Ankara, Turkey. From that vantage point he observed events not only in Turkey but also in Iran, Lebanon and Cyprus. In 1959 his base of operations was moved to Cairo, where he watched the progress of Nasser from "positive neutralism" to positive "Arab socialism." Mr. Walz was in Yemen right after the revolution that ousted Imam el Badr, and during his Middle East assignment he traveled extensively over the immense area ranging from Istanbul to Mogadiscio and from Tripoli to Teheran.

Born in South Bend, Indiana, Mr. Walz was graduated from the University of Notre Dame. He began his career in journalism as a reporter for the South Bend *News-Times* and in 1935 became a reporter for the Washington *Post*. Eight years later he joined the staff of *The Times,* serving with its Washington bureau until he went overseas. He is now posted in Ottawa as *The Times'* Chief Correspondent in Canada.

He and his wife, Audrey, have collaborated on two historical novels, *The Bizarre Sisters* and *The Undiscovered Country*. The Walzes have two sons.

THE MIDDLE EAST

A NEW YORK TIMES BYLINE BOOK

The Middle East Crossroads

A FEW WEEKS after I arrived in Turkey in the spring of 1958 to take up my new post as a Middle East correspondent of *The New York Times,* I flew from Ankara to Istanbul to cover a "routine" meeting of the heads of state of the Baghdad Pact nations.

At Yesilkoy Airport I found the red carpet rolled out across the tarmac and the presidential band standing at attention, instruments poised to strike up the national anthem of the next arrivals—King Faisal II of Iraq and his Premier, Nuri as-Said. The plane from Baghdad was overdue. The band waited and so did President Celal Bayar of Turkey and Premier Adnan Menderes. . . .

As so often happens in the Middle East, plans

proved to be subject to change at the last moment. For the plane from Baghdad never arrived. The King and the Premier never left home. Army rebels staging a coup d'état caught them, and before it was over they were dead. A band of pronationalists (and for the moment pro-Nasserist neutralists) took power and one of the Arab monarchies was abruptly ended.

Three days later I was in Beirut, Lebanon, where in a rapid turn of events United States Marines were landing. They were there to make sure that the pro-Western President, Camille Chamoun, did not share the fate of the Iraqi leaders. Lebanon had been in a state of armed rebellion for several months.

Thus I observed the Middle East "in crisis" from the beginning of a six-year tour that also saw revolution in Turkey (1960), when Premier Menderes in turn met his death; the drastic nationalization stage of the Nasser revolution in United Arab Republic (1961) and its dramatic follow-up, the secession by coup d'état of Syria from Egypt (1961); the revolution in Yemen (1962), and a second coup in Baghdad that ousted the 1958 revolutionary, General Abdul Karim Kassim. Meanwhile the Arab "war" with Israel continued periodically to stir and alarm the Middle East.

These events provided correspondents on the scene with an almost continuous succession of "good stories." But personally I was sorry that my dispatches, along with the rest, probably contributed to the popular impression that the Middle East is a bubbling stewpot, a chronic "crisis area."

Most outsiders do not appreciate—indeed, do not know—that 100 million people who live in the Middle East experience the same hopes and fears that we do. They have the same ambitions and despairs. They share our eternal faith that good works will bring about a better world. Why are such people caught up in so much bitter, apparently unending strife?

One reason, I am convinced, is that outsiders— from East and West—have done a good deal to keep the Middle East in turmoil. Foreigners may not be responsible for the area's backwardness and poverty, but they are heavily accountable for its strife and disunity. The Middle East has never been isolated and it has rarely been allowed to work out its own problems.

The Middle East is still a great crossroads. Jet airliners on global schedules touch down at Istanbul, Beirut, Teheran and Cairo at all hours of the day and night. The huge modernistic air terminals do business in languages spoken all over the world. These are the jet-age caravans and caravansaries, and the Middle East, as it has done for centuries, watches the intercontinental traffic, with all its wealth, come and go.

On the sea approaches to the Suez Canal, ships

line up—as many as 75 a day—for the north and south convoys. Oil from the Middle East itself contributes to a commerce of such riches as Marco Polo and the Venetian merchants never dreamed of.

All this has intensified the world's interest in the Middle East and the desire on all sides to influence and control the area's people. Thus, a revolution in Iraq in recent years landed U.S. Marines on the beaches of Beirut. Gamal Abdel Nasser's seizure of the European-owned Suez Canal brought on an invasion of Egypt by Britain, France and Israel. The creation of a Jewish national state in the Middle East started a war that the United Nations has yet to settle. Even the overthrow of the tyrannical Iman of Yemen, one of the most backward and poorest of countries, caused convulsions in capitals far away.

The following chapters will try to explain what the Middle East is and why it seems so "crisis"-prone.

I

Islamic Empire

THE MIDDLE EAST is at the hub of the land masses of Europe, Asia and Africa. If one journeys through its countries clockwise from the north, one starts with Turkey, moves east through Syria, Iraq and Iran, south through the Arabian Peninsula, taking in Jordan, Saudi Arabia, Yemen, a series of petty sheikdoms and the British colony of Aden, west to Egypt and Libya and finally north along the eastern Mediterranean coast to Israel and Lebanon. Although the whole area is grievously short of drinkable water, it fronts on several great seas— the Mediterranean, Black, Red and Caspian—and also on the Persian Gulf and the Indian Ocean.

The area is rightly called the "Cradle of Civilization." It was the center of the ancient world. A succession of cultures grew up there while much of the continents all about was in a primitive or savage state—even Europe being at most in the Stone Age. All the famous empires of antiquity rose and fell in the Middle East—the Sumerian, the Babylonian, the Assyrian, the Hittite, the Egyptian and the Persian. Later, in the fourth century B.C., came the Macedonian Empire of Alexander the Great to dominate the whole Middle East. In Alexander's footsteps the Roman Empire followed, although it never succeeded in conquering Persia.

When Rome fell before the northern barbarians, the Eastern Roman, or Byzantine, Empire carried on for another 1,000 years. But long before its final collapse it began crumbling. Its great southern provinces were a hodgepodge of peoples and cultures ruled by a rigid governmental apparatus. Christianity had been largely enforced by imperial decree and it was divided by bitter schisms. This restless, turbulent area, inhabited by Greeks, Syrians, Phoenicians, Egyptians, various tribes of Palestine and many Jews, became the heart of perhaps the most spectacular conquest in history.

This conquest began in the seventh century after Christ in the Arabian peninsula near the Red Sea. There lived from 570 to 632 an Arab, Mohammed. Religious fervor gave him a vision and a message. To achieve his ends he used the sword and the Arabic language.

Arabic speech is full-bodied and strong. It is, in addition, eloquent and rich. It has produced fine lyric poetry and superb narrative, as we know from *The Thousand and One Nights*. It also carried Islam, the religion of Mohammed, to the far corners of the then-known world in an extraordinarily short time—less than 100 years.

The Koran is the book of Islamic teaching. To the Moslems—those who embrace Islam—Allah, the one God, is the source of all life. Through his Prophet, Mohammed, and the Koran, Allah is the fountainhead of compassion, charity, faith, honor and a world of brothers. Mohammed, however, did not interpret God's compassion as a command to turn swords into plowshares. Believers were taught that the highest honor was to die on the battlefield of the Holy War.

Mohammed became a military leader as well as a judge and lawgiver. At Badr, near Medina, his political capital, Mohammed led 300 Moslems in a rout of 1,000 Meccans. This victory was regarded as proof that God backed Mohammed's religious mission.

The Moslem fighters carried on this mission after the Prophet's death. In the seventh century they spread out in every direction open to advance by land. They pressed north through Syria and Anatolia to the Bosporus. Eastward they overran Mesopotamia and Persia (now Iraq and Iran) and the

greater part of Afghanistan and Turkestan. Westward, crossing the Sinai Desert, the Moslems con-
quered Egypt and the whole northern coast of
Africa. Traversing the Strait of Gibraltar, they took
Spain and Portugal and pushed over the Pyrenees
into France as far as Avignon, Carcassonne and
Bordeaux.

The conquerors took with them the Arabic language no less than their religion. In fact, the language spread faster than did the religion—although
the religion, when it gradually caught up with the
language, tended to stay longer.

Both the language and the religion lost out in
Europe, where such architectural monuments as
the Alhambra are the only remaining traces of the
Moslem invasion. In Turkey and Iran the religion
stayed without the language, although Arabic script
is used in Iran to this day and was used in Turkey
until 40 years ago. There are today millions of non-
Arabic-speaking Moslems throughout Southeast
Asia, including Indonesia.

However, from the middle of the eighth century
until the rise of the Ottoman Turks early in the
16th century, there existed a Moslem-Arabic empire
larger than Rome's at its height. Then the Ottomans, having taken Constantinople with another
army of Islamic warriors, introduced Turkish rule
which held the Moslems, excluding the Persians but
including the Arabs, together for 350 years—or

until modern times.

But before the Ottoman conquest the Arabs had their most enduring experience in unity: the Crusades of the 12th and 13th centuries.

The Middle Eastern Moslems have never understood the Crusades as Western Christians know them. To Moslems the French Raymond, the Rhenish Baldwin, the Sicilian-Norman Tancred, the English King Richard the Lion-Hearted were not Crusaders out to preserve the Christian holy places, but marauders.

After Godfrey of Bouillon, supported by Raymond and Tancred, took Jerusalem on July 15, 1099, there was wholesale slaughter. "The heaps of heads and hands," records a Latin chronicler of the time, "could be seen through the streets and squares."

The Moslems had established a long record of tolerance about use of the holy places in Jerusalem. Many of the holy places were their own. The Dome of the Rock, from which Mohammed is believed by his followers to have ascended on his one-night flight to heaven, is hardly more than a stone's throw from the Christians' Way of the Cross and the Church of the Holy Sepulcher marking the site where Christ was buried.

Christians, Jews and Moslems had always intermingled in Jerusalem. Moreover, Christians and Jews served as high officers in various Arab states.

More than likely the vizier one encounters when reading *The Thousand and One Nights* is a Jew.

The onrush of Crusaders determined to "rescue" the Holy Sepulcher came as a shock to the Moslems. Suddenly they were confronted by rude, barbaric people from far away—men who did not wash or wear silks or walk on fine carpets as civilized Arabs did. What were such strangers doing in the Holy Land? It made no sense to the Arabs. They could think of nothing they had done to annoy them.

What the Arabs did not know was that a frenzied urge to make warlike pilgrimages to the Holy Land and take it from the "heathen" had spread across Europe like the plague. It started with repeated appeals from Alexius Comnenus, the ruler in Constantinople of Christian Byzantium. He asked for help from the Christian West to repel the Seljuk Turks, who, he said, were overrunning his territory and threatening his capital.

His appeal was answered by Pope Urban II in a speech in 1095 that recited stories of presumed Moslem atrocities. He urged Christians to "enter upon the road to the Holy Sepulcher, wrest it from the wicked race and subject it." The Pope spoke in southern France near territory taken by the Moslems. A France on edge because of the Moslem advances took up the cry, and within two years 150,000 Franks and Normans were in Constanti-

nople ready to "free" Jerusalem. Soon they were
joined by columns of marchers and by sea expedi-
tions from countries across Europe. Antioch, Tyre,
Tripoli and other points fell to the Crusaders, who
set up outremer kingdoms—domains beyond the
sea.

The story of the Crusades is a long and fascinat-
ing one that has attracted writers of history and fic-
tion for centuries. The Christians succeeded in taking the main "holy" objectives, but they bickered
over spoils and prestige. Some forgot all about their
"holy mission" after setting themselves up with
castle and court.

Sooner or later the mightiest sovereigns of Europe
joined a Crusade. Philip Augustus of France, Fred-
erick Barbarossa of Germany and Richard the
Lion-Hearted took part at one time or another.

But the alarmed Arab Moslems resolved to end
the invasion. They grew stronger as they drew together, and gradually the crusading spirit shifted
from the Christians to the Moslems. And at the head
of this rally was the Moslems' greatest hero—Saladin, a Kurd from Mosul, in Mesopotamia, who
had grown tall, learned and elegant and was
even to make friends with Richard the Lion-
Hearted.

Saladin, who appears as a most sympathetic figure in Sir Walter Scott's *The Talisman,* stopped the
Crusaders. He "freed" Jerusalem from the Chris-

tians and is remembered for his leniency to the con-
quered. There was no slaughter as there had been
when the Christian Godfrey captured the city.

Saladin united through his person the Syrian
throne of Damascus and the throne of Egypt, which
he had won. In Cairo he built the citadel that still
stands, commanding a sweeping view of the city,
the Nile and the Pyramids on the far horizon. Of
Saladin Professor Philip K. Hitti, the Arabist of
Princeton University, has said: "The champion of
Islam became and remains the paragon of Arab
chivalry in Islam and Christendom."

Today Gamal Abdel Nasser, the hero of millions
of Arab nationalists, likes to think of himself as a
modern Saladin. "He drove the first European imperialists and colonialists from our midst," Nasser
has declared to a visitor. The eagle on Saladin's coat
of arms is, in modernized form, the official ensign
of Nasser's United Arab Republic.

The unity achieved by the Arabs in the Crusades
was not disturbed importantly by the Ottoman
Turks during their conquests. These Turks, after
taking Constantinople in 1453, carried Islam to
Greece and the Balkans and pushed to the very
gates of Vienna before being pushed back.

The crust of Turkish protection had good and
bad effects on the Middle Eastern Arabs. It caused
them to be let alone and they were not molested by
the West again for a long time. But, isolated, they

did not benefit from any cultural exchange during the post-Renaissance period when Europe forged ahead so dramatically.

The Middle East, safe in its Islamic cocoon, remained essentially what it had been at the beginning of the 16th century. It retained its language, its manners and its way of thinking. *Insha'allah* (God willing) and *malish* (never mind) continued to be key words in the Middle East's leisurely life. If something did not get done, *malish,* tomorrow is another day, *Insha'allah.* If anything goes wrong, if the locusts get the harvest, *malish,* that's fate. Never hurry—it's too hot and it makes no difference. So take a rest.

Europe used the astronomy it was taught in the Middle East. It used the tempered steel, the cane sugar, the damask (from Damascus), the muslin (from Mosul) to help create a new world.

The Middle East slumbered on. It grew backward, inefficient, its kingdoms corrupt. But it was unified.

II

The Western Powers Move In

WHEN GAMAL ABDEL NASSER SPEAKS, as he often does, of Saladin as the trumpeter of the modern Arab awakening, he is not altogether accurate. As we have noted, the Arabs slumbered undisturbed for about 600 years after the Crusaders left.

Nor did the Arabs waken of their own accord. It was the Europeans, again, who aroused them. Specifically it was Napoleon, whose army arrived in Egypt in 1798 to cut the British off from India. Bonaparte failed in his main purpose, but he shook the Arab East. Its isolation ended. It has not been the same since.

Along with his troops Napoleon brought with him to Egypt about 200 savants—scientists of all kinds, historians, artists and artisans. They investi-

gated and recorded everything they observed about
Egypt—its antiquities, its climate, its flora and
fauna, its water (especially its river, the Nile). Their
report, *Description of Egypt,* was an exhaustive
work: 24 volumes of text, charts, tables, maps and
beautiful engravings of the fine Directoire period.

When it was published in France, academicians
scoffed that so many thousands of pages had been
devoted to describing one place. "What country is
worth such a Nile flood of material?" they asked.
But the influence of *Description of Egypt* was
enormous. It opened up tremendous activity in
archaeology, antiquities, geography and natural resources that persists to the present day. Directoire
and later Empire furniture, for example, blossomed
into a display of sphinxes, obelisks, scarabs and
other Egyptian decorative motifs.

The science of archaeology had its real beginning when a young Frenchman, Jean François
Champollion, succeeded in deciphering the Rosetta
Stone, a basalt slab inscribed in hieroglyphic, de-
motic Greek and classical Greek. This stone, discovered by one of Napoleon's soldiers in Rosetta, a
village at the mouth of one branch of the Nile,
eventually became the key to knowledge of Egyptian antiquity.

When the French had to surrender in Egypt, the
British victors considered as part of the spoils of
war not only the Rosetta Stone but also the savants'

great report. The savants defiantly said they would destroy their work before letting it go to the English, who must then be answerable to the world for the vast body of knowledge lost. Faced with such resistance, the British took the Rosetta Stone, now in the British Museum at London, but permitted the French to take to Paris their magnificent record of Egypt.

Thus European interest in the Middle East was vitalized anew.

At this time all the modern states of the Middle East except Iran and certain southern Arabian sheikdoms were held by the Ottoman Sultanate, the empire seated in Constantinople. This empire embraced what is now Turkey, Syria, Iraq, Lebanon, Israel, Jordan, coastal Saudi Arabia, Yemen, Egypt, Libya and the island of Cyprus. It even extended beyond the Middle East into Greece, the Balkans and parts of Russia. In North Africa it included what was to become Algeria.

Among the officers in the Ottoman force sent by the Sultan in Constantinople to help the British evict Napoleon was a young and ambitious Albanian Turk named Mohammed Ali. In Egypt he did little to get rid of Napoleon, but once Bonaparte was gone he founded a dynasty that lasted until the Nasser revolution of 1952. The dynasty came about when the Ottoman Sultan made the governorship of Egypt hereditary in Mohammed Ali's line.

Mohammed Ali and his successors looked to the West, and the story of their reigns is a serial account of European-Egyptian exchange at all levels —military, economic, cultural and scientific. European specialists followed Napoleon's savants to Egypt and Mohammed Ali sent Egyptians to Europe for education and training. Today we would call it an early form of technical assistance and the Arab nationalists would call it infiltration of "imperialists" and "colonialist exploiters."

Nevertheless, under the stimulation and pressure of this 19th-century interchange, important developments took place, and the nationalism and restlessness that swept the Middle East in the 20th century was undoubtedly a result.

A sizable role in the intellectual awakening of the Middle East was played by British, French and American missionaries. Roman Catholic priests and nuns from France went to Lebanon and Egypt, where there were Christian communities that needed schools and religious guidance. Lebanon, as a matter of fact, has long had a Christian majority and still does officially, although this is now disputed by the Moslems, who are increasing more rapidly than the Christians. And in Egypt today Christians constitute a little less than 8 per cent of the population.

Protestant missionaries, physicians and teachers went to the Middle East with the avowed aim of converting Moslems—something no longer permitted by most Moslem governments. The Protestants also founded a number of secular schools. Robert College, established in 1863 in Constantinople (now Istanbul), developed a strong engineering faculty. The Syrian Protestant College in Beirut (now the American University in Beirut), founded in 1866, established over the years medical, pharmaceutical, nursing, public health, engineering, agricultural and other schools. American Presbyterians set up primary and secondary schools in Egypt. Later the American University in Cairo came into being with strong faculties in liberal arts and Oriental studies.

These American universities in Istanbul, Beirut and Cairo have continued to operate with supervision and financing from the United States, but they are increasingly an anomaly in their environment of nationalist education and nationalization of private institutions.

In Egypt the successor to Mohmmed Ali who took Western-style modernization most seriously was Ismail, who reigned from 1863 to 1879 and was granted the title of Khedive (Viceroy) of Egypt by the Ottoman Sultan in 1866. Ismail introduced the first postal system in Egypt and gave

Cairo running water. He installed the telephone and the telegraph. Above all, he completed and opened the Suez Canal, although his extravagances finally cost Egypt control of it.

The canal was really the idea and achievement of a foreigner, Ferdinand de Lesseps of France. The French Government blew hot and cold on the project and the British definitely opposed it because it would enable France to divide an area of increasing British concern and interest.

Eventually de Lesseps won the interest of Ismail's predecessor, Said Pasha. But, throughout, only de Lesseps had confidence that further development of steamboats would make useful a canal cutting 100 miles through the Sinai Desert to link the Mediterranean and the Red Sea. Such a canal could not be used, it was argued, by northbound sailing ships. These were frequently becalmed in the Red Sea, and in a canal there would be no room to maneuver against adverse winds.

With this argument the British pressed the Sultan in Constantinople, the nominal overlord of Egypt, to oppose the canal, and frequently Said Pasha would find it expedient, if not necessary, to hold back money he had promised de Lesseps.

After great difficulty de Lesseps managed to raise from private stockholders in Britain and France the funds Said Pasha had held back. There is no question that the Suez Canal—probably the

biggest engineering enterprise since the Pyramids
—was the accomplishment of one man—de Lesseps.

In the course of construction Said Pasha died
and was succeeded by Ismail, who the British
thought would be more amenable to pressure. But
once in power Ismail worked harder for the canal
than had his predecessor.

The great waterway was opened with pomp and
ceremony in 1869. The Khedive built a palace in
Cairo for his guest of honor, Empress Eugénie of
France, and her court. He commissioned an opera,
Aïda, from Giuseppe Verdi, and to present it he
built in Cairo the first opera house in the Moslem
world. (It is still in use and the original *Aïda* sets
and stage effects are preserved in the property
room.)

Unhappily, Khedive Ismail, promoting so many
worthwhile enterprises, went deep into debt and to
extricate himself incurred obligations abroad.
Through a maneuver with the Rothschild bankers,
Disraeli, Britain's Prime Minister, bought up all the
Khedive's canal stocks. The British and French
found new reasons for interfering in the Khedive's
affairs. Finally, in 1882, the British, on the pretext
of helping Ismail's successor put down a revolt,
moved in with occupation forces. They stayed 70
years.

It was not the first time England had taken a

piece of the Ottoman Empire by offering help in a crisis. Britain kept Russia from imposing harsh terms at the end of the Russo-Turkish War, but Turkey in return had to cede Cyprus to Britain in 1878.

In both cases—Turkey and Egypt—Britain was primarily interested in protecting water routes—the Bosporus and the Dardanelles in Turkey and the Suez Canal in Egypt. Both were important to a great sea power with interests all over the world.

Meanwhile other European powers did their bit to take the Ottoman Empire apart. In North Africa the French occupied Algeria in 1830 and Tunisia in 1881. Algeria remained a French territory until the end of a bitter revolutionary war in 1962. Tunisia, for many years a French protectorate, received independence in 1956.

Italy, dreaming of a place in the African colonial sun, took over the Ottoman province of Tripoli in 1911 and claimed as a colony the whole of the territory that is now the Kingdom of Libya. During the nineteen-twenties and nineteen-thirties Mussolini spent millions of dollars there in an effort to settle overcrowded Italians in the sparsely populated Bedouin country. But Italians never migrated in large numbers. Thirty years afterward houses built for Italian settlers dot the lonely countryside east of Benghazi. The Libyan Government tries without much success to move its nomadic Bedouin tribesmen into those structures, but the Bedouins prefer their tents, and the camels, though not averse to indoor accommodation, find the ceilings too low.

After World War II Libya was made an independent kingdom by the United Nations. It is ruled by the ascetic King Idris, leader of the Senussi, one of the most conservative sects in Islam. His principal problems today, beyond those of age and ill health, are the unification of his people and the proper investment and spending of the large funds derived from Libya's recent oil discoveries.

The fragmented Ottoman Empire collapsed after the First World War. The finish came when the Ottoman Turks made the fatal mistake of siding with the Germans.

During the war Britain encouraged the restive Arab subjects of the Ottoman rulers to revolt and promised them independence if the Turks and Germans were beaten.

This revolt in the desert—graphically chronicled by Lawrence of Arabia—helped Britain march up from Egypt and take Palestine and Damascus. But the Arabs, having helped, found their territories divided up by the peacemakers—not into independent states but into something new called "mandates." This they still regard as a great betrayal of all they had been promised.

The idea of the League of Nations in forming mandates after the disruptions of the First World

War was to prepare the way for the independence of peoples unready for it. Peoples—in this case, the Arabs—were backward by all Western standards. They were largely illiterate and, having slumbered under the rule of overlords for centuries, they had no experience in self-government. The League of Nations, therefore, devised the "mandate," in which some well-established power would offer temporary protection, guidance and instruction. The "mandates" would become fully independent states as soon as they showed they could stand and walk. That was the concept.

The League intended the mandates to be something novel, something entirely different from colonies or occupied territories. That the European powers—Britain and France—should sometimes confuse their new role of foster parent with their old role of colonialist might have been expected. And they did.

This is not to say that the role would not have been difficult in the best of circumstances and with the best of intentions. As it turned out, the Arabs never understood why the British and French were there, and suspected the worst. The European commissioners in charge of carrying out mandates frequently gave the Arabs reason for misunderstanding and fear.

Under League of Nations aegis, Palestine and Iraq became mandates of Britain, and Syria and

Lebanon wards of France.

The struggle that ensued was long and complicated. It lasted through the period between the world wars. Eventually the British and French got out and the mandates became independent states, now members of the United Nations. But it cannot be said that the noble purpose of the "mandate" exercise—to lead backward peoples to happy freedom—was ever achieved.

The Arabs felt that in Palestine the British showed more concern for their commitment to the 1917 Balfour Declaration than to the progressive well-being of the Arab majority there. The Balfour Declaration said in terms too uncertain ever to be clear of controversy that Britain intended to help the Zionists establish a Jewish "national homeland" in Palestine.

The Arabs opposed this idea from the start—on the ground that Palestine was the homeland of nearly a million Arabs whose ancestors had lived there for many centuries. The Palestine Arabs, accordingly, resisted until the day the British left in 1948 after having turned over a partitioned mandate, not to the Palestine Arabs, but to the Zionist Jews for the new State of Israel.

In Iraq the British were able to obtain more collaboration. After uprisings in 1920 the pro-Western King Faisal, leader in the desert revolt, came to the throne. He led the country through a relatively peaceful decade, after which the League of Nations recognized Iraq as an independent state. The monarchy lasted until July, 1958, when nationalists bitterly opposed to the Western involvements (particularly the Baghdad Pact) of young King Faisal II, the old monarch's grandson, led a coup cutting down both the King and his pro-Western Premier, Nuri as-Said.

Transjordan was separated from Palestine in 1921 in what the Arabs regarded as an attempt of the "Europen imperialists" to divide and rule. What was first an emirate became the Hashemite Kingdom of Jordan, propped up by British military support and American economic aid. King Hussein, the young ruler, tries hard today to maintain a neutralist standing with such revolutionaries as the United Arab Republic's Nasser and successive Algerian leaders. But he would fall in a day without British and American financing. Appropriately, he has titled his book on his life and experiences *Uneasy Lies the Head*.

The French had almost continuous trouble with the politically astute and worldly-wise merchants of Syria. There were disturbances from the start, including strikes and armed attacks. Damascus was bombarded more than once. The French commissioners had a way of growing impatient and increased their restrictive measures as affairs went from bad to worse. They tried censorship and the imprisonment and exile of troublemakers. All of this, far from suppressing the Syrians, inspired them to new efforts toward nationalism.

In Lebanon the Christian majority (the only one in the Middle East) and a tradition of French education, speech and thinking made it easier for the French guardians. The Lebanese, who strike one as traders first and Arabs second, were amenable to French association, whether in banking or women's fashions.

Lebanon prospered and enjoyed better schools and public administration than other foreign-controlled territories in the Middle East. She was accorded her independence in 1943, and Syria won hers in 1945. The Syrians and Lebanese still celebrate the day the French departed and spend the rest of the year coping with problems left behind by their former French masters.

Britain's withdrawal from the Middle East is still far from complete. The British not only support Jordan militarily but also maintain bases in Cyprus, independent since 1960, and Libya. In Aden there is not only a base but also a colony, and a British-sponsored federation of sheikdoms exists in what the Arabs call "occupied Yemen."

Arab resentment of the Western powers is rooted in the "betrayal" following World War I. The United States was and is an ally of the countries that, in Arab eyes, betrayed a solemn promise to give the Arabs independence and freedom—terms they frequently confuse with Arab union or Arab unity.

So their leaders still distrust all Western powers. The Soviet Union escapes this distrust for the simple reason that it has never been a colonial master in the Arab East.

III

A Middle East Soldier
Defeats the West

ON A HILL overlooking Ankara the pink marble
tomb of Ataturk is under the eternal vigilance of
select members of the Presidential Guard. In a
downtown square a heroic equestrian statue of
"The Father of the Turkish Republic" watches over
the capital he established in the heart of the Anatolian plain.

Almost every office and living room in Ankara
has a portrait of Ataturk. He appears in the various
poses of a soldier-statesman. Sometimes he stands
tall and lean in the puttees and khaki of World War
I uniform. Again, he is in Western civilian dress.
His portraits show him to have been in his prime a
handsome man on the scale of movie heroes. He
had sharp, slightly slanted eyes (they were blue),

high, broad cheekbones and graying hair combed severely back.

In his later years this Middle Eastern soldier developed his passion for Western culture to the extreme of wearing on formal occasions top hat, white tie and tails. There hung in the British Embassy in Ankara a full-length portrait of Ataturk in this formal attire. Nearby was a matching portrait of Queen Elizabeth II. As a British journalist and I passed these pictures one day, he said to me: "Ataturk looks as though he had just arrived to escort the Queen in to dinner."

And well he might, had he lived a little longer. For, having trounced the West on the battlefield and secured Turkey's independence, Ataturk turned his Eastern country fully around to face the West and drove it into step with Western progress.

In a little less than 20 years Ataturk led the Turks on an almost incredible march. As a leader he set an example for other Eastern soldier-revolutionaries: first the late Riza Shah of Iran and more recently Egypt's Nasser. None of his emulators, however, has matched the ferocious single-mindedness of the son born to a Turkish customs clerk in the town of Salonica in 1881.

Mustafa Kemal, as he was named in boyhood, went from a military academy to the War College in Constantinople at a time when it was a center of underground opposition to the repressive Ottoman

Sultan Abdu-l-Hamid II. Speaking later of his years as a cadet, Mustafa Kemal recalled:

"I worked well at the usual lessons. On top of this, new ideas emerged among some of my companions and myself. We began to discover that there were evils in the administration and politics of the country, and we felt the urge to communicate this discovery to the thousands of students of the College. We founded a handwritten newspaper for them to read. We had a small organization in the class. I was in the committee, and I used to write most of what appeared in the paper."

But from the earliest days of his military career Mustafa Kemal was in fact a snarling lone wolf. He snapped at men he regarded as beneath him, though often they were his superiors. He spoke out against the "evils" he found about him, regardless of where he was or who was within earshot. He lost his temper over the corruption of Constantinople, the subservience of the Ottoman Sultanate to the Western powers and the indifference of Islamic authorities to the ignorance and backwardness of the peasants.

Inevitably he was soon arrested but emerged from a few months' detention to be posted, perhaps half-exiled, to the staff of the Fifth Army at Damascus in Syria. In 1907 he was in Macedonia, promoted to major.

His biographers believe he played a part in the

reformist and strongly nationalist Young Turk movement, but there is little evidence that he got along well with its leaders, since after the Young Turk revolution of 1908, which led to the ouster of Sultan Abdu-l-Hamid but not of the Sultanate itself, he did not emerge as a prominent figure.

Instead he turned to military matters exclusively. He translated two German manuals on combat drill. He made a trip to Europe for the famed French military maneuvers. He fought in the 1911–12 war with Italy, which resulted in the loss of Libya, and in the 1912–13 Balkan Wars, in which Ottoman Turkey lost nearly all her remaining territory in Europe. Later he served as military attaché in Sofia, Bulgaria.

He asked to return to Turkey in 1915 for active duty in World War I and was placed in command of a "paper" 19th Division on the eastern shore of the Sea of Marmara. There was nothing imaginary about his performance, however, for when the British opened their campaign against Constantinople by invading the Gallipoli Peninsula, Mustafa Kemal was there. Selecting the right promontory to defend at the right time, he moved (without high-command orders) the troops he needed to drive off the British, saved Constantinople and found himself a hero. The Allies never regained the initiative there. The Gallipoli victory was the only important success of the Ottomans in World War I.

Mustafa Kemal was given the rank of general, but was dispatched to eastern Turkey. The Young Turks, then in power, expected things might be more difficult for him in that region. However, he won victories against the Russians at Bitlis and Mus.

In the fighting in Syria and Palestine during 1917 and 1918 Mustafa Kemal served with distinction. But no particular honors came to him, partly because of differences with the German general under whom he served, Erich von Falkenhayn, and partly because of ill health.

In September, 1918, he was among the Turkish and German forces pushed back by General Allenby's British offensive. Mustafa Kemal was organizing a last counteroffensive north of Aleppo, Syria, when the armistice on the Eastern Front was signed. He arrived in Constantinople on November 13, the day the Allied fleets steamed up the Bosporus.

The Western powers planned at the end of World War I not only to take over Ottoman Turkey's remaining empire but also to cut the heart out of Turkey herself. They intended, first, to give Constantinople and the entire Bosporus-Dardanelles waterway back to the Greeks—after 500 years.

Thousands of Greeks had, of course, remained in Turkey during those 500 years. All cities in western Turkey, notably Constantinople, then the capital, and Smyrna (now Izmir), the seaport on the Aegean Sea, had largely Greek populations. The Greeks were usually the important traders—the shippers, importers and shopkeepers. The Turks in Turkey were mostly peasants in the villages of Anatolia and Thrace.

The Greeks had, in fact, been in what is now Turkey since before the time of Homer, whose *Iliad* narrates their adventures there during the Trojan War. The whole Aegean area today is strewn with the magnificent ruins of Greek civilizations that were old when the Romans arrived.

The Turks, who were eighth-century latecomers to this historic region, not surprisingly developed a resentment and jealousy of the Greeks, partly because they were there first and partly because the Greeks, who stayed on, usually managed to lord it over the Turks. Dominating the great seaports, the Greek merchants grew wealthy at the expense of the Turkish peasants who tended their flocks and wrested harvests from the harsh Anatolian plain. (Anatolia, sometimes called Asia Minor, comprises 97 per cent of present Turkey.)

When the Ottoman Empire lay dying, the Greeks were determined to return to Turkey on a grand scale and permanently. Their postwar leaders won the sympathetic ear of the Allied peacemakers. On December 8, 1918, Allied troops occupied Constantinople. When General Franchet d'Esperey of

France arrived on the following February 8 to take command, he rode a fine white horse, the gift of the local Greeks.

Allied forces, already in possession of the Ottoman Empire's Arab provinces to the south, now moved north into Turkey. French soldiers from Syria marched into Cilicia and Adana. British units occupied the Dardanelles, Samsun, on the Black Sea, and Ayntab. They also took over the entire railway that had been built years before by the Germans.

In April, 1919, the Italians landed at Antalya, a beautiful little Mediterranean port nestling against the Taurus mountains. It was understood in Allied councils that Italy would receive certain southern regions of Anatolia.

To Sultan Mehmed Vahideddin the Allies all about him seemed not so much a threat as a good means of subduing and destroying the Young Turk leaders who, starting out as reformers, had grown strong as dictators and had taken much of the power out of the Sultan's hands. They had been responsible for allying the Ottoman Empire with Germany during the war and, of course, could not remain in control after the Allied peace. The Sultan had no way of knowing that the events now overtaking the Young Turk leaders would also destroy him and put an end to the Turkish Sultanate itself.

On the Sultan's side, or so it seemed, was the

apathy of the exhausted and low-spirited peasants. They seemed indifferent both to the fate of the Young Turks and to the invasion by Allied forces. But they were not entirely demoralized and it took the Greeks, the long-time bane of their existence, to prove it.

A Greek army landed at Smyrna in May, 1919, and this the Turks could not bear. The Italians had landed and so had the French and the British, and these the Turks had let pass. Greeks, however, were another matter, for, once entrenched in Turkey again, the Greeks would surely never leave. Eleutherios Venizelos, the Greek Premier, had, in fact, laid claim to the Aegean regions of Turkey at the peace conference. And it was well known that the Greek Government was ambitious to restore around Constantinople the once-glorious Greek Christian Empire (Byzantium, which had finally expired in the 15th century).

This threat awakened and aroused the Turks. In Constantinople there were protest meetings. In Anatolia guerrillas sprang up to harass the Greek army, which, having occupied Smyrna, began moving east. The angry Turks awaited only a leader to fight off this ancient enemy.

That leader was, in fact, already on the way.

Mustafa Kemal arrived at Samsun May 19, 1919, on a curious mission considering the role he was about to play. The general, who had returned

from Palestine frustrated, discontented and rebellious a few months before, was now under orders
to move into eastern Anatolia and disband remaining Turkish forces. The Sultan feared they might
prove troublesome and reportedly took satisfaction
in giving one of the most effective potential troublemakers the job of disarming them.

Learning at Samsun that the Greeks had just
landed in western Turkey, Mustafa Kemal acted in
direct opposition to the Sultan's orders. He began
organizing a movement and an army to support his
dream of "Turkey for the Turks."

As Mustafa Kemal, at 38, began the climactic
and most dramatic military campaign of his career,
it is proper to note that he was moving toward the
first nationalist success in the modern Middle East.
The Sultan was against nationalism because he
held it responsible for the disintegration of the Ottoman Empire. He wanted nationalist activity sup-
pressed and his own troops disbanded even though
the Allied invaders were every day violating the Armistice and the Greeks, the ancient enemy, were on
his back.

In Samsun, Mustafa Kemal felt free of Constantinople, which he regarded as decadent, and
breathed the invigorating air of Anatolia, where he
detected signs of national awakening. He immediately set to work organizing and coordinating resistance groups. He prepared to defend the Turk-

ish plain against foreign invasion.

To Constantinople's alarm, Mustafa Kemal established a "representative committee" in Ankara, an ancient hill town in the center of the bleak plateau about 300 miles east of the Bosporus. Ankara became resistance headquarters and later the capital of Mustafa Kemal's independent Turkey.

The young general was right when he thought the Turkish peasants could be mobilized. As he moved against the Armenians, the French and the Greeks, not to mention the Sultan's forces, he had behind him not only the rag-tag-and-bobtail peasants but also their women.

In a war of independence that lasted nearly three years Mustafa Kemal became the George Washington of his country. Like Washington, he displayed rare military acumen and a genius for handling poorly armed and untrained troops. As the independence army moved south and west Mustafa Kemal was desperate for weapons and ammunition. From his only source, the Black Sea port of Samsun, peasant women hoisted supplies to their shoulders and carried them on foot over the mountains and plain to their fighting men.

At the battle of the Sakarya River, not far from Ankara, the Turks under the personal command of Mustafa Kemal decisively defeated the Greeks, who then began a tragic retreat. The Turks, pressing after them, found Turkish villages burned and

Turkish women and children dead. Enraged, the Turks poured into Smyrna crying for vengeance. As the Greeks tried to evacuate this virtually Greek city, the advancing Turks fell upon them and the climactic battle of the War of Independence ended on September 9, 1922, in a bloody massacre.

With the Greeks driven out of Turkey, Mustafa Kemal completed the conquest of Anatolia for his nationalist movement and deposed the Sultan. The peace conference at Lausanne, Switzerland, in 1922–23 established the independence of Turkey. Mustafa Kemal had thus made Turkey, the seat of the old Ottoman Empire, the only defeated power in World War I to have rejected the terms imposed on it by the Western victors, terms that would virtually have destroyed Turkey as a national state had they remained in force.

Turkey was now free, but the fight for modern life was yet to begin. To move ahead, Mustafa Kemal took a most unexpected course. Having beaten off the Western overlords by force of arms, he now turned to the West for example. "Civilization means European civilization," he declared and, addressing the National Assembly in 1924, remarked: "The Turkish nation has perceived with great joy that the obstacles which constantly, for centuries, had kept Turkey from joining the civilized nations marching forward on the path of progress have been removed. . . . The nation has finally decided to achieve, in essence and in form, exactly and completely, the life and means that contemporary civilization assures to all nations."

The Turkish nation, of course, had made no such decision. Mustafa Kemal had made it for the nation and, often against powerful and sometimes popular opposition, he had effected and was to effect by sheer force of personal will many drastic, far-reaching reforms.

He separated religion and government so that no longer would the head of the Moslem community be the political ruler, as the Sultans had been for centuries. In Mustafa Kemal's view, the duality of the Sultans' role had been responsible for the corruption of officials and the ignorance and indifference of the people to that corruption. To emphasize the separation of religion and government he moved the political capital from Constantinople, later renamed Istanbul, to Ankara in 1923.

In the same year, on the argument that modern, civilized government must be a government by the people, he declared Turkey a republic and became its President. The old Caliphate, the Sultans' spiritual and temporal administration, was abolished in 1924 and a new constitution was adopted.

Mustafa Kemal subsequently changed the whole legal system, hitherto Islamic. A new civil code, adapted from the Swiss, replaced the old religious laws, even in such practices as marriage and divorce. Under the civil code a couple entered matrimony with equal rights for both the man and the woman. Shockingly to many, it became possible for a Moslem to marry a non-Moslem and for adults to change their religion if they wished. Under the old religious laws a married woman had had few rights and seldom asserted those she possessed against the will of a husband, father or brother.

Mustafa Kemal ordered the men of Turkey to wear Western-style hats in place of the fez. This may seem a trivial "reform" to a Westerner, but to a Moslem it was a profound change, for the red fez with its black tassel was a last symbol of Moslem identity. Many men of wealth and station in Constantinople wore the fez even though they had already adopted Western-style jackets and trousers. But Mustafa Kemal said the fez must go because "it sat on the heads of our nation as an emblem of ignorance, negligence, fanaticism and hatred of progress and civilization."

The prohibition of the fez, however, was as nothing compared with the edict that women must throw away their veils.

"In some places," Mustafa Kemal declared in a speech in 1925, "I have seen women who put a piece of cloth or a towel or something like it over their heads to hide their faces, and who turn their backs or huddle themselves on the ground when a man passes by. What is the meaning and sense of this behavior? It is a spectacle that makes this nation an object of ridicule."

About the same time he abolished the old Ottoman calendar and introduced our Gregorian system of dates. He also established the 24-hour "international" clock as the official and only approved measurement of time.

Lastly he persuaded the National Assembly to approve an order abolishing Turkey's Arabic script and adopting the Latin alphabet. This changeover would seem a most formidable undertaking that should have required years, perhaps a generation, to accomplish. But Mustafa Kemal accomplished it in a matter of weeks. It required a careful phonetic application of Latin letters to the sounds of Turkish speech.

Addressing members of his Republican People's party, Mustafa Kemal said: "We must free ourselves from these incomprehensible signs [Arabic script] that for centuries have held our minds in an iron vise. You must learn the new Turkish letters quickly. Teach them to your compatriots, to women and to men, to porters and to boatmen. Regard it as a patriotic and national duty. Our nation will show, with its script and with its mind, that its place is with the civilized world."

Thus within a short five years Mustafa Kemal forced the Turks of the New Turkey to give up their Sultan and Caliphs, their Holy Law, their traditional apparel and their Arabic script—all in the name of "civilization."

Of course he did not achieve this without resistance and in some cases rebellion. The city Turks in Constantinople and Ankara had made many Western contacts and generally welcomed the changes. But vast majority of Turks, the village peasants, had to be taught first of all what Mustafa Kemal was driving at and why. The wonder is not that he encountered much resistance but that in a day before radio, motion pictures and other means of mass communication and modern education were known in Turkey, he got the response he did.

Mustafa Kemal died of a complication of diseases in 1938. Parliament by decree had given him the surname of Ataturk—Father of the Turks. And that is the name he is known by today.

A generation after his death every one of his reforms remains in force, but they have not accomplished all that Ataturk said or thought they would. The adoption of the Latin alphabet, for example, has not put an end to illiteracy.

Visitors to Turkey today observe in the villages many signs that the reforms are not in universal operation. Women in the villages still cling to their veils. One suspects that in many cases they do so as a protection against the responsibilities of the equal rights that Ataturk wanted them to have.

Many educated Turks of the younger generation think the time has come to update the reforms and apply them on the broader scale made possible by radio, motion pictures, schools and clinics. Birth control, it is suggested, should be used to relieve the "uncivilizing pressures" of a 3 per cent annual population increase.

But many present-day young Turks also ponder whether Ataturk's sense of urgency did not drive him, and Turkey, too hard too fast. He uprooted old ways and customs and planted in their place a "hothouse culture" that leaves Turks wondering where they are and who they are.

If you ask them, most Turks will say they are not Middle Easterners at all but Europeans, although 97 per cent of their country lies in Asia. "We don't merely wear Western clothes," they say. "We are allied with the West. We belong to the North Atlantic Treaty Organization and the Central Treaty Organization. We are not neutrals like the Arabs. Never mistake us for Arabs."

Certainly Ataturk's Westernization drove the Turks out of the fold of their Arab neighbors— Moslem though they all may be.

Ataturk made the Turks see the world and he set them up as self-respecting citizens of an independent country with the ambition to make it some day wholly, economically and politically, free.

IV

Oil and the Wheels of Progress

THE PRESENCE OF OIL in the Middle East has been known since ancient times. It was a mineral that would burn—but to what purpose? It is probable that natural gas, finding its way to the surface of the earth, played a role in the history of oracles.

But oil as a resource was through the centuries an insignificant item compared with gold, silver and precious stones. In classical times there was much more demand, say, for olive oil—used for food, cooking and anointing—than for any greasy substance seeping out of the ground.

Underground oil—or petroleum—awaited modern uses. Even techniques of production and exploitation had to be developed with modern tools. In the United States the discovery of petroleum in

Pennsylvania in 1859 led immediately to nothing more dramatic or revolutionary than the switch from whale oil to kerosene in the lamps of New England. To the whaling industry that was a profound change, but the value of oil was not truly appreciated until years afterward when inventors developed the combustion engine. This made possible the motor age—the age of the automobile, the diesel engine and the airplane.

Today oil has revolutionized civilization. It energizes our industry and transport. Wars are waged to possess it, and it enables us to fight wars more fiercely than our ancestors could have imagined.

What would have happened to the Middle East's oil if Western powers had not become interested in it and moved in to take it out is a matter of speculation. Most of it would have remained undiscovered and undisturbed, and much good and evil in the Middle East would not have arisen.

Several Middle Eastern countries would have remained vastly poor. They would not have stirred the envy of their (so far) oilless neighbors. The whole Middle East might not be the contentious center of world exploitation that it is and will be until all its oil is used up or has become obsolete as fuel.

The British were the first Westerners to become interested in taking Middle Eastern oil in quantity. In 1889 one of them obtained a major concession from Shah Nasr ed-Din of Persia to exploit minerals in the whole of that country. The contract signed with Baron Julius de Reuter, a British national, stipulated that he could take anything from the ground that he wanted except gold, silver and precious stones. He was to have a monopoly for 60 years, and as an expression of good faith he had deposited 40,000 pounds sterling—about $200,000 at that time—with the Shah's treasury. Later it was agreed that he would pay the Persian Government 16 per cent of the profits from the company's operations.

Of this concession Lord Curzon wrote that "when published to the world, it was found to contain the most complete and extraordinary surrender of the entire industrial resources of a kingdom into foreign hands that has probably ever been dreamed of, much less accomplished in history."

What made the concession even more extraordinary was that it caused no great excitement either in Persia or Britain, although Russia criticized it. The Persians' Middle Eastern neighbors paid small attention to it, those who even heard about it.

Today, in contrast, Iran, as Persia was renamed in 1935, is not overly happy to have a contract with an international consortium that gives the country 50 per cent of the profit from oil sales, yielding in 1965 more than $300 million. Saudi Arabia and Kuwait receive more than $500 mil-

lion annually. Iraq, Bahrein, Qatar and Libya are
now also oil-producing lands earning millions. Syria, Lebanon and Jordan all derive revenues from
oil-transporting pipe lines. Egypt, a small producer, reaps more than $160 million a year in tolls
from tankers using the Suez Canal to carry Middle Eastern oil to Europe.

Petroleum production in the Middle East has
risen from slightly more than 6.3 million tons in
1930 to 200 million tons in 1964. The Middle East
has 60 per cent of the world's known oil reserves.
In the last 10 years it has become the major single
supplier of oil in the international market. Europe,
which used to import heavily from the Western
Hemisphere, including the United States, now de-
pends almost entirely on the Middle East. The
area's revenues from oil now approach $2 billion a
year.

In almost every Middle Eastern country where it
has been discovered, oil has drastically affected
political life. In Iran a dispute over nationalizing
the petroleum industry in the early nineteen-fifties
led to a flight from the country by the present
Shah and the ultimate overthrow of the nationalist
leader, Dr. Mohammed Mossadegh, who opposed
him.

Mossadegh was the first Middle Eastern leader to
propose nationalizing a national resource—the oil
that was enriching not only the British sharehold-

ers of a British company but also the British Government itself.

European demand for oil had doubled and tripled during the years of economic recovery after World War II. Noting this, Iran, then the largest Middle Eastern petroleum producer, sought to increase her royalties from the Anglo-Iranian Oil Company, which held a monopoly on Iran's oil operations. The company offered to improve Iran's share of the profits, but the concessions were deemed insufficient by a Government under increasing pressure from the National Front, led by the fiery Mossadegh. Extremists in the front demanded nationalization of the petroleum industry as part of a drive for the "liberation" of Iran from foreign influence.

In 1951 the Iranian parliament, yielding to the front, enacted an oil nationalization bill. This immediately set off a series of strikes and disturbances in the oil fields of southwestern Iran. Two Britons were killed and the British Government ordered naval maneuvers in the Persian Gulf.

Shah Mohammed Riza Pahlevi's moderate, pro-Western Premier, Hussein Ala, tried one compromise after another. He proposed making the company Iranian property and leaving production and distribution operations to foreign experts, including company technicians. But Mossadegh's nationalists would have none of this. On April 28, 1951, the young and unsure Shah reluctantly asked the radical Mossadegh to take over as Premier.

For political reasons Mossadegh proceeded at once with nationalization of oil. But his difficult project, for which there was no precedent in the Middle East, was complicated by the disruptive activities of Communists. Demonstrations, strikes and other disturbances continued and the company closed its plant in Khuzistan.

In short order, production stopped, martial law was declared and the Tudeh (Communist) party, although officially outlawed, found it easy to gather 30,000 angry Iranians at a mass meeting in Teheran, the capital, to shout anti-Western slogans and display pro-Soviet placards.

Mossadegh's problem, aside from shutting up the Communists, was to open up the "nationalized" oil plants and wells. In the next two years of crisis he succeeded in doing neither.

It soon became apparent that a nationalized industry in Iran might produce petroleum but it could not transport it to market and sell it. And the British refused to perform these essential tasks in the circumstances. Iran's economy came to a standstill and Mossadegh pleaded for American aid.

President Truman and later President Eisenhower remained officially neutral but tried to persuade Mossadegh and the British Foreign Secretary, Herbert Morrison, to negotiate. The Iranian

Premier, desperate and ill, came to Washington for help and conducted negotiations for more than two months from a sickbed in Walter Reed Hospital.

The company not only refused to distribute Iranian oil but also went to the World Court to keep Mossadegh from concluding oil sales with Japan and Italy. These never worked well and Mossadegh, far from winning friends, was isolated and his country neared financial collapse.

The Shah tried to discharge the Premier and, not succeeding, fled with his queen by private plane to Baghdad and Rome. As he had hoped, his departure set off new riots and demonstrations in his favor. The popular feeling was that Mossadegh had gone too far in defying the Shah and should no longer be trusted with the country's destiny. He and the nationalization of oil had brought Iran to chaos.

On August 19, 1953, Mossadegh surrendered to General Fazlollah Zahedi, whom the Shah had appointed the new Premier. A few days later the Shah returned triumphantly to his throne.

General Zahedi started Iran's return to normalcy by renewing the request for United States aid, and this time President Eisenhower, who had refused help to Mossadegh, promptly authorized a $45 million emergency grant-in-aid and $23.4 million for technical assistance.

With the exit of Mossadegh (to his farm north-west of Teheran, which he has ever since been permitted to manage but not to leave) went all plans for Iran's running her own oil business. The public by this time was not so pro-nationalization as it was anti-British. So the Government solution was to turn over the exploitation of oil to an international consortium. It is made up of more than a dozen companies. A British-Dutch group, including the British Petroleum Company, which had been the Anglo-Iranian Oil Company, holds 54 per cent of the stock, an American group holds 40 per cent and a French group 6 per cent. The consortium operates on the 50–50 profit basis—half for itself and half for Iran—that has become the standard throughout the Middle East.

The Mossadegh crisis dramatized the dispute that has existed since oil became a commercial enterprise in that part of the world.

The Anglo-Iranian Oil Company had operated as a business venture in which it considered it took considerable risk. It had signed a contract with Iran to guarantee certain revenues and stood to enjoy profits from its successful operations and management. When this venture turned out far better than had been expected, that was so much capitalist good fortune. According to the company, a contract was a contract, to be upheld and respected by both parties. This view was argued not only by the company but also by Foreign Secretary Morrison of the British Labor party Government and later by his successor, the Conservative party's Anthony Eden, as well as by Britain's Sir Gladwyn Jebb before the United Nations Security Council.

Moreover, had not British enterprise and expertise brought new wealth to Iran to a total of 150 million pounds sterling by 1950? Had not the British Government rendered financial, health and education services for which the backward Iranians should be grateful?

Instead the Iranians, like other Middle Easterners, made it clear that they did not see contracts as Westerners did. Contracts were drawn to serve a purpose and the Iranians contended, should neither outlast the purpose nor remain in effect if the purpose was not served. The purpose of the Anglo-Iranian contract was, from the Iranian point of view, to guarantee income, not to create tremendous profits for foreigners. If the company had risked capital and contributed experts and advanced techniques, it need not be rewarded quite so lavishly—with profits ranging up to 150 per cent, according to the Iranian figures. After all, Allah had given the oil to the Iranians—not to the British.

Iran also complained that she lost revenues when the company sold oil to the British Navy at a secret low price and paid income taxes to the British Government before calculating Iran's share of the profits. In fact, in 1950, the year before nationalization, the taxes that the company paid to the British Government were three times the oil royalties paid to Iran. Finally, Iranians thought they should hold more good company jobs and accused the British of being too slow at training them for technical posts.

The establishment of the consortium amounted, however, to a victory for the Anglo-Iranian Oil Company, whose stock climbed the day the arrangement was announced from 5 pounds sterling per share to 18 pounds. The defeat of Mossadegh also convinced Foreign Secretary Eden of Britain that he could, by taking a tough stand, bring down any Middle Eastern leader bent on nationalization. This undoubtedly influenced him during the Suez crisis three years later.

Britain decided during World War I that Iraq, or Mesopotamia as it was then known, was important to her strategically. English prospectors found strong indications of oil around the old Turkish districts of Mosul and Kirkuk. With the support of France, Britain insisted before the League of Nations that she have a mandate over Mesopotamia with the oil area on her side of Iraq's new border. She insisted to the point of threatening war against Ataturk and his resurgent Turkey, which claimed Mosul and Kirkuk.

Ataturk was either unaware of or uninterested in oil deposits at that time. But he contended that Turkey should have jurisdiction over all non-Arab areas of the defunct Ottoman Empire. Mosul and Kirkuk were inhabited by Kurds, an independent non-Arabic mountain people. Nevertheless, British pressure in the League of Nations and on Ataturk himself was strong enough so that the boundary line was drawn straight through Kurdish territory. Today, therefore, some Kurds are in Turkey while others are in Iraq, where they have long been at odds with their Arabic overlords in Baghdad. But the oil around Mosul and Kirkuk stayed in Iraq. In 1921 the British installed a monarch there, King Faisal, an Arab prince who had hardly ever seen the country before.

All these manipulations by a Western power bent on control of a big oil deposit laid down a delayed fuse for events which were to disturb the Middle East long after the Turkish-Iraqi boundary had been settled.

Iraqi oil, unlike that in other Middle Eastern areas, welled up a long way from the sea. It had to be carried to the Mediterranean through pipelines across to Haifa in Palestine and Tripoli in Lebanon. During the Palestine war of 1948 Arabs cut the Haifa pipeline. In fact, the transportation difficulties were such that the British-controlled oil com-

pany has never intensively exploited the Iraqi oil
fields.

What money did come into Iraq from oil sales
benefited the common people very little. Also the
Iraqi royal house never cleared itself of the charge
that it was dominated by the British. These two
facts were largely responsible for the overthrow of
the Iraqi monarchy by Gen. Abdul Karim Kassim
and his nationalists in 1958. General Kassim was
in turn overthrown and executed in 1963 because
of popular discontent based partly on his costly war
with the rebellious Kurds. The present republican
(nationalist) Government under President Abdel
Salam Arif has made, at this writing, what is at best
an uneasy and possibly short-lived peace with those
hardy mountaineers. Iraq can never be sure of the
full consequences of a European-drawn boundary
that gave her oil and at the same time sovereignty
over unruly and headstrong Kurds.

During World War I the newly invented tanks,
the primitive planes and the battleships of the Allies ran on American oil. American reserves were
shockingly depleted. When the war was over, the
United States not surprisingly took an interest in the
new Persian and Mesopotamian oil fields with a
view to acquiring a share in them but was virtually
squeezed out of both areas by Britain.

Because Englishmen had never found oil in the great Arabian peninsula, the Foreign Office in London did not interfere when King Ibn Saud took over the rule of most of that vast, sparsely settled desert. London was not particularly aroused when the King granted concessions to an American oil company in return for an immediate $150,000 "depression" loan. The traffic of Moslem pilgrims to Mecca that year, 1933, had been poor.

The Standard Oil Company of California obtained in fact a 60-year concession covering a huge area. The operating company was called the California Standard Oil Company and a year later, when the Texas Company joined in the enterprise, the name was changed to the Arabian American Oil Company, or Aramco. It has since developed into one of the world's greatest oil production and distribution companies.

Petroleum was discovered in commercial quantities in Saudi Arabia in 1938 and rich wells were brought in surprisingly soon—at Dhahran, Dammam, Abqaiq and Abu-Hadriya. Production rose steadily through World War II, from 580,000 barrels in 1938 to 21,311,000 in 1945. In that time King Ibn Saud's oil revenues rose from $166,890 to $4,820,000 a year.

The King was highly pleased. Aramco gave him good reason to be. It paid him his royalties and never asked how he spent them. It employed an increasing number of Arabs in drilling operations and the construction of roads, pipelines, houses and other facilities. Moreover, Arabs were not only employed but also trained for technical posts. The company built hospitals, clinics and health centers in the oil-production and refinery areas.

King Ibn Saud developed a friendly relationship not only with Aramco but also with the United States, something that had not happened before in the Middle East because the United States had never previously been a presence there. This friendship reached a climax in February, 1945, when President Roosevelt, returning from Yalta, received Ibn Saud aboard an American warship in the Suez Canal. The two talked—not about oil but of Palestine. The King received assurances from the President of the United States that he would "take no action" in his official capacity "which might prove hostile to the Arab people."

Developments in Palestine within two years led the Arabs to question the meaning of the American assurance. But this never interrupted the flow of oil from Saudi Arabia through Aramco channels.

By 1950 Saudi Arabia, producing 25 million tons, was second only to Iran as the Middle East's principal oil producer. She has since outstripped Iran, although she is now second to Kuwait. Her annual revenues are more than $500 million.

Like other Middle Eastern producers, the Saudi

Arabians now feel they should enjoy a better arrangement than the 50–50 division of profits always accorded them. But the real problem faced by the present monarch, King Faisal, a nephew of Ibn Saud, who died in 1953, is that of spreading the $500 million to $600 million of annual wealth. Faisal, since dethroning his elder brother, King Saud, in 1964, has stated several times that he is aware that oil revenues should be used not to provide the royal family with fleets of gold-plated air-conditioned Cadillacs but to raise living standards for Saudi Arabia's six million people. The royal family is now limited to only $38.4 million a year!

Faisal was nudged into this point of view because his subjects had heard over their transistor radios of nationalist revolutions in Egypt and Algeria, of popular uprisings in Syria and Iraq and of a genuine spread-the-oil-wealth welfare program in Kuwait.

Little Kuwait, nestled in a corner of land at the head of the Persian Gulf, provides the Cinderella story of Middle East oil. Not so long ago a writer for the magazine *Foreign Affairs* entitled an article on this country "Kuwait: A Super-Affluent Society." And so it is after having traveled the road from rags to riches in the quarter-century since oil was discovered there.

Other Arab lands would have a hard time emulating Kuwait, which has no such excessive population as Egypt, no such stretches of desert as Saudi Arabia, no such medieval backwardness as Yemen. Kuwait is compact. Its population is only about 320,000. Oil receipts are so large that the annual revenue (from oil alone) amounts to more than $3,360 per inhabitant. All this revenue does not reach the average Kuwaiti, but under the enlightened rule of Sheik Abdullah al-Salim al-Sabah all Kuwaitis now have access to schools, hospitals, clinics, community centers, roads and housing.

The Sheik may not be the world figure that some other Arab leaders are, but his city-state domain offers the outstanding exhibition of good works from oil. Moreover, through the Kuwait Fund for Economic Development of the Arab Countries, with capital resources of nearly a billion dollars, the Sheik is making economic development loans to other Arab states, including some, like Saudi Arabia, that have plenty of oil wealth themselves. In early 1965, the Sheik placed nearly $100 million at the disposal of Nasser's United Arab Republic when it was desperately hard pressed for "hard" currency.

Oil operations in Kuwait have been carried out to a great extent by British capital and enterprise. This has not produced the friction and crises that British control evoked in Iran and Iraq. Perhaps the great concentration of petroleum in Kuwait, with easy access to sea lanes, made the task of exploitation less troublesome. The promptness of the Sheik in using his wealth for the common good must have played a beneficial role. And undoubtedly the responsiveness of the Kuwaiti Arabs to a life totally unknown to them two generations ago has been a major factor.

However, Kuwait is the exception. There it is oil or nothing. If the oil economy vanished, there is no way Kuwait could survive by developing industry or agriculture. This the other Middle Eastern oil countries might do—if they have the will.

In them, in well-ordered circumstances, oil would lubricate the wheels of progress. The immediate effect of depending on oil wealth has probably been to undermine the ambitions of countries that possess it. There is less incentive to industrialize in Iran and Iraq, although the Shah of Iran is making valiant efforts in his land, than in non-oil countries such as Turkey and Egypt. There is also less effort to improve agriculture when it is known that petroleum revenues are available for schools, hospitals and roads.

Libya, which has only recently struck oil, has a northern plateau with fine farming possibilities, but Libyans are abandoning good growing land to drive trucks for new oil companies. Iraq does not begin to work all her available arable land or use fully her fine water resources. Jordan, however, having wistful hopes of oil but none in reality, is making hard-won improvements in land development.

For the Middle East oil wealth may be a boon, but it is not always a blessing.

For the United States, with its large vested interest, Middle Eastern oil has become a big factor in foreign policy. If the West, including the United States, does not exploit and provide the market for petroleum products, who will? Certainly the Soviet Union or Communist China would step in to try to do so.

The United States, with limited reserves, cannot afford to let Middle Eastern oil go by default to other hands. It is not just a matter of American investment; national security is involved. Even President Kennedy, who went to great pains to pursue a middle course between Israel and the Arabs, made it clear that the United States must look after its petroleum interests. Nasser was told in 1963 that while the United States had recognized the new revolutionary Government in Yemen, which Nasser was backing with several thousand troops, it would not support him in any attack on Saudi Arabia, which was supplying arms and money to the forces of Yemen's overthrown Imam.

Finally, oil in the Arab countries affects United States policy in the Arab-Israeli dispute. Since World War II successive Administrations, whether Democratic or Republican, have sought to recognize the claims of both sides. The United States was the first to recognize Israel diplomatically, and has supported it with millions of dollars in aid. Yet Washington, like Moscow, backed Egypt in the 1956 crisis when Israel joined Britain and France in an attack on the Suez Canal. The record, however, shows that were it not for American interests in the Arab Middle East—meaning oil in the Arabian peninsula and its transit through the Suez Canal—United States policy would probably be more pro-Israeli than it is.

V

The Creation of Israel and the War with the Arabs

THE CREATION of Israel by the United Nations in 1948 was one of the great dramas of modern times. The long-cherished dream of "The Jewish Homeland" in Palestine has been a reality for almost two decades. Yet the Arab-Israeli dispute still persists and clouds the historical fact that Arab and Jew, far from being congenital enemies, are ethnological relatives. Both are Semitic and in ages past got along well together. Arabs and Jews complement each other. The Jewish drive, love of organization and aptitude for concentration on any given task can have a place in bringing progress to the Arabs' relaxed way of life. And yet one can see how Jewish efficiency and organization injected forcibly into the Arab world at a time of rising nationalism could be the lighted fuse of a stick of dynamite.

It is tragic that the Holy Land, which has been the heartland of Judaism (and of its offshoot, Christianity) and Islam, is today divided into hostile camps. Jerusalem is bisected by a wall. Israel, to remain in existence, must engage in a bitter struggle with neighbors as suspicious, envious and resentful as only Arabs can be.

At this writing the Middle East is under the threat of a new flare-up because of the prodding tensions between the Arabs and Israel. Once more it is not mere border incidents that provoke the turmoil but rather political complications involving distant states.

Nasser learned in late 1964 that West Germany, one of his principal sources of economic and technical aid, was giving Israel $80 million worth of arms. In retaliation he quickly invited Walter Ulbricht, the leader of Communist East Germany, which West Germany does not recognize, to make a goodwill visit to Cairo. He also hinted he might be ready to extend diplomatic recognition to East Germany. West Germany, in hopes of appeasing Nasser, stopped its arms shipments to Israel, but it canceled its economic aid to the United Arab Republic the minute Ulbricht set foot on Egyptian soil in February, 1965. It also announced its readiness to recognize Israel, and the Knesset, Israel's parliament, setting aside memories of the wartime slaughter of Jews in Nazi Germany, accepted West Germany's offer of diplomatic ties.

The Arab reaction was violent. Mobs attacked West German properties in Lebanon, Iraq and Yemen. And Nasser called on all Arabs to break relations with West Germany if it carried out its announced intention to exchange ambassadors with Israel.

Since 58 countries have diplomatic representation in Israel, including the United States and several nonaligned nations sympathetic to the Arab cause, and many of these also have embassies in Cairo and other Arab capitals, such a furor may seem incredible. But not to anyone who knows the background of the Arab-Israeli conflict.

The idea of a Jewish homeland in Palestine was an old one. Pogroms (mass killings) and persecutions around the world inspired longings for Jewish freedom and independence in the land of the Old Testament Israelites. In the 19th century there were migrations, especially from Russia, where waves of anti-Semitism led to pogroms. The first Zionist colony of Russian émigrés was set up in Palestine in 1882. Baron Edmond de Rothschild gave money and the Jewish Colonization Association was established to buy land for Jews migrating from Europe.

Zionism, the movement for reconstituting a Jewish nation, received its first important impetus, however, with the Balfour Declaration of World

War I, when Arthur James Balfour, the British Foreign Secretary, put his Government on record in favor of "the establishment in Palestine of a national home for the Jewish people."

Not all Jews have favored the idea of a Jewish national homeland. Many non-Zionists are opposed to the political cast of Zionist nationalism. They hold that Judaism is a religion, not a nationality. Some sided with the Arabs from the start against the formation of a Jewish nation in the Middle East. Accordingly, the militant efforts of Dr. Chaim Weizmann, the Zionist leader, to obtain a pro-Zionist declaration from the British wartime Government was not supported by all Jews.

The voices of Dr. Weizmann and his many followers were, however, heard in the highest councils in the years to come in Britain and the United States and ultimately in the United Nations.

In the era between the World Wars, when Britain administered Palestine under a League of Nations mandate, Jewish immigration proceeded rapidly. From a 1922 figure of 83,790, the number of Jews in the territory grew to 528,702 in a total population of 1,739,624.

Moreover, the Jewish immigrants, mostly from Europe, brought with them their highly developed sense of organization. They formed political parties. They showed a bent for collective farming, organizing agrarian settlements. They established cooperatives for banking, insurance, marketing and buying, transportation and irrigation.

But a mere statement of facts cannot adequately depict the drama of the migration of Jews to Palestine. The rise of Hitler in Germany in 1933 started an exodus, and the stream of "unwanted" people to the British mandate territory swelled rapidly.

Some German Jews who had been able to dispose of their property gave up to the common cause all they owned on arrival in Palestine. Gradually, as Hitler's terrible pogrom took effect, Jews considered themselves fortunate to escape with their lives. These arrived in Palestine in the nineteen-thirties with nothing at all—not even, in many cases, their health. Among the arrivals were broken, battered people with only their courage and belief in a homeland to sustain them. How emaciated victims of Nazi concentration camps endured the long, cruel journey of escape and what they accomplished when they reached the homeland constitute an epic.

These people set to work—in a land largely desert, in a hot climate to which they were not adapted —building a model state. It was their children, growing up in health and freedom, who composed an army whose emotional drive the Arabs in 1948 could not counter.

The Arabs have never appreciated what Israel meant to Jews. They sensed only that something "dangerous" was occurring and that some day it might prove disastrous.

The Arab majority in Palestine remained as they were—highly unorganized. Their community life was wrapped up in the old practices of the Supreme Moslem Council that controlled the religious courts and the *Waqfs,* or charitable endowments. There were no Arab political parties, no Arab coopera-tives. Many Arabs were Bedouin nomads who roamed the Negev beholden to no one but Allah. While the Zionists were pumping in large amounts of financial aid from Europe and the United States, the Arabs were getting none at all.

Unrest grew in the nineteen-thirties. When the exodus of Jews from Hitler Germany brought new waves of immigration to Palestine (60,000 arrivals in 1935 alone), anti-Jewish riots erupted. The Brit-ish found their mandate increasingly onerous, and in 1937, after deciding that Jews and Arabs could not live together in peace, a Royal Commission pro-posed that the mandated territory be partitioned.

The outbreak of World War II in 1939 led to a paper truce, but disturbances persisted. The Zionist leaders, losing faith in British ability to control the situation when the war would end, turned to the United States for help. They were listened to with sympathy by Presidents Roosevelt and Truman.

The British plan to partition Palestine was one of the first important controversies to come before the United Nations. The plan was a gerrymandering attempt to separate predominantly Jewish communities from Arab communities. The result was a contortion almost impossible to describe without a map. Roughly the new Jewish state was to be given northern Palestine except for a pocket fronting the Lebanese border. The Arab state would get the central and eastern area from Afula down to Beersheba, including Jerusalem and Bethlehem. The Arabs would also get a strip on the Mediterranean from Gaza to the Egyptian border. The Zionist state would get the Negev with the port of Aqaba on the gulf leading to the Red Sea.

On November 29, 1947, the United Nations General Assembly approved the partition motion by a vote of 33 to 13 with 10 abstentions. It is interesting today to note that the United States and the Soviet Union joined in voting for partition. So did France. Britain, because of her mandate, abstained, as did some Latin-American countries and Ethiopia. In voting against partition—and the creation of a new Jewish state—the entire Arab bloc was joined by the Moslem lands of Afghanistan, Iran, Pakistan and Turkey as well as by India, Cuba and Greece.

The Arabs' reaction was exactly what might have been expected. As they saw it, the far-off outside world, predominantly Western, had forced something on the Middle East it did not want.

In accordance with the U.N. resolution, the British terminated their mandate and the last British forces withdrew on May 14, 1948. A National Council, set up in Tel Aviv to establish a Government, immediately proclaimed the Jewish State of Israel. A few hours later President Truman affirmed the birth of the nation by extending to it United States recognition.

The Arabs have never forgotten this or forgiven Truman. They remind visitors at every opportunity that both Roosevelt and Truman had promised never to commit the United States to a decisive course in the Middle East without first obtaining the consent, if not the approval, of the Arabs as a party vitally concerned. They recall that President Roosevelt gave such a promise only three years before to King Ibn Saud when they met in 1945.

Moslems, generally, were stirred to resentment because they were one of the few peoples without a history of discrimination against Jews. Mohammed told his followers that they must always show consideration toward the people of The Book—that is, Jews and Christians, whose Bible was the Prophet's source book. Mohammed had heard all the famous Bible stories from Jewish merchants at Mecca. The great Biblical figures from Abraham to Jesus all appear in the Koran. During the Middle Ages and on to modern times, while Christians persecuted Jews, Moslems allowed them to live in peace and even hold high public office. Yet, in Moslem eyes, Moslems' land was now given to the Jews by a Western world suffering from a guilty conscience for its failure to intervene when Hitler perpetrated his monstrous pogrom.

Arab armies moved into Israel from all sides. On the face of things these forces should soon have overwhelmed the infant state. Israel's Arab neighbors all had established armies. The Egyptian Army was British-trained. The Arab Legion of Transjordan, now Jordan, was commanded by Brigadier John Bagot Glubb, a Briton. Iraq had a substantial force and Syria and Lebanon had small standing armies supplemented by volunteer forces.

But the war didn't work out the way the Arabs thought it would. The Egyptian Army's bad ammunition and worse food, a result of corruption in King Farouk's court, caused it to lose heart. The Transjordanian force under Glubb Pasha made a better showing but would not join hands with the Egyptians. The Iraqis were too far away. The Syrians and Lebanese did not put up a serious fight. The Israeli forces pushed the Arabs back on almost every front.

Israel emerged victorious, for the armistice brought about by the United Nations must be considered an Israeli triumph. Israel won because its small army was tightly organized, high spirited and well equipped. It had Western efficiency.

With the armistice Israel held control of three-fourths of Palestine, far more than it had been granted by the partition. Moreover, the war had displaced 70 per cent of the Arab population of 1,320,000, leaving the Jews in the majority.

Whether these Palestinian Arabs were forced out, as the Arabs claim, or departed of their own volition, as the Israelis insist, they became—these one million refugees—tragic political pawns. Israel refuses to readmit them or compensate them for loss of property. The Arabs, except for Jordan, will not accept them as citizens, since to do so would amount to a partial settlement of the "war" with Israel. The refugees, whose numbers grow larger because of a rising ratio of births over deaths, remain after all these years wards of the United Nations. They live in camps maintained by the U.N. in Lebanon, Syria and Egypt.

The United Arab Republic, in refusing to accept the refugees as citizens, contends they are nationals of an Arab state of Palestine, whose government President Nasser has set up at Gaza. It will assume control, he says, over all of Palestine when Israel is destroyed and that territory is no longer "occupied." He could not, if he wanted, find room for the refugees in his own overpopulated country.

Jordan never recognized the Gaza "refugee" government. The Palestine land west of the Jordan River held by the Arab Legion was annexed by Jordan in 1948, right after the armistice, and a few months later its inhabitants became Jordanian citizens.

While there had not been universal support for the Zionist cause, the United Nations vote for the creation of Israel settled the matter for everyone except the Arabs. The United States, and Americans individually, soon began pouring in immense quantities of aid to help the Jews develop Israel. No one can deny that Israel used that help to good advantage. The Israeli success in itself can account for a substantial part of the Arab suspicion, resentment, and fear.

Since its birth Israel has shown the dynamism that its people, immigrating from more than 80 countries, including most of the Arab lands, had exhibited previously. There were about 600,000 people in Israel when the state was created; today there are approximately 2,250,000 Israelis, including 250,000 non-Jews who are mostly Arab Moslems.

Israel has introduced a highly socialized but Western-oriented and democratically elected government to the Middle East. It has tackled desert reclamation aggressively and with its foreign-aid resources has earned the right, though not exclusively, to the slogan: "We made the desert bloom." Israel has built up an impressive reservoir of technological skill and, to the annoyance of Nasser, has exported it to underdeveloped African and Asian countries that the Egyptian leader aspires to claim as his own sphere of influence. United States technical assistance to Israel (but not other forms of American aid) ended in 1962. Israel has made Middle Eastern countries—notably Turkey and Iran, though hardly the Arab lands—aware of its sense of mission.

David Ben-Gurion, who for many years was Israel's indomitable Premier and articulate philosopher, always insisted that the new Zionist state must not only attract Jews from all over the world but also "make a lasting contribution to world history."

Discussing this with Gertrude Samuels of *The New York Times Magazine* on his 75th birthday, Mr. Ben-Gurion, then Premier, said: "I think the greatest contribution we can make is to build a model society which will lift humanity to greater heights, if copied in other countries. . . . Africans and others are coming to study our agricultural settlements, our ways of cooperation, our youth and labor movements. They see the way we are 'melting' people into a united, civilized nation. . . . You have before your eyes here many examples of the pioneering spirit. We have more of that type proportionately than any other people. The pioneering is very much alive, and not only in the collective farms, but also in our institutions of learning. Our scientists are pioneer scientists who search for ways to exploit solar energy, to de-salt sea water, in order to utilize deserts and to increase energy. That pioneering research could open wider horizons for all mankind."

The Arabs, of course, do not see Israel in so bright a light. In their opinion the Zionists should not be doing whatever they are doing on land that, far from being a "Jewish homeland," had been in Arab hands for centuries. From the beginning they have considered the Israelis to be, as Nasser so frequently states, "foreigners foisted on us by Western imperialists." And Nasser adds: "They do not belong here, nor do we intend to tolerate them long."

Where and when will it all end? I believe no end is yet in sight.

The Arabs refuse to sit down at a peace conference with Israeli leaders, since to do so would imply they recognize Israel's right to the territory the Arabs still call "occupied Palestine." There were rumors in 1956 that Nasser was considering a discreet contact with Israel through the United States to look for a peace settlement. Of this a shrewd Arab politician said: "I wish it could be done so we could get back to normal life, but not even Nasser could dare risk that. No Arab leader could do it and live." King Abdullah of Jordan was assassinated in the Holy Place of Jerusalem on July 20, 1951, because, it was said, he was merely suspected of favoring negotiations with Israel.

While Israel has offered to talk peace with Arab leaders, she has not opened the door wide to fruitful negotiation. She says she cannot repatriate the Palestine refugees because they are by now all "brainwashed" by Nasser. Nor has Israel offered otherwise to implement broadly the 1954 United Nations resolutions calling on Israel to permit the Palestine Arabs to return to their homes or receive compensation for lost property. The Israeli attitude is that the Arabs left voluntarily, that they were not forced to go. The Arabs; of course, deny this.

Israel's very successes, and especially her growing Jewish population and the Zionists' call for ever more immigrants, make the Arabs bristle.

Thus peace seems still as remote as the end of the rainbow. I feel it will never come during the lifetimes of the present bitter antagonists. David Ben-Gurion, at this writing nearly 80, has passed the chair of Israeli power, at least momentarily, to perhaps more flexible leadership. However, Nasser, who during his lifetime must, in all probability, be a party to any Arab-Israeli peace, is only 48. Moreover, he began a new six-year term as President in 1965.

VI

Another Middle East Soldier "Liberates" His People

AMONG the few Egyptian soldiers who fought well against Israel was a young major, Gamal Abdel Nasser, who had long been disgusted with the subservience of his king, Farouk, to the British in Egypt. When Farouk's corrupt henchmen profiteered by supplying the troops on the Israeli front with bad food and faulty weapons, Nasser and a small group of other military men began to plot the monarch's overthrow.

These officers, whose hard inner circle numbered 12, toppled Farouk on July 23, 1952, in a coup d'état that surprisingly was without bloodshed. The people of Cairo, turning on their radios that morning, heard that the Government had been taken over during the night by the National Revo-

lutionary Council, of which Bragadier General Mohammed Naguib was the head. Three days later
Naguib called on King Farouk at the royal summer palace in Alexandria and persuaded him to
board his yacht with whatever belongings he could
pack by nightfall and sail for exile in Europe. Farouk departed and Naguib returned to Cairo to become the nominal leader of the new revolutionary
regime.

Farouk's exile and the end of the Alid dynasty
were never the cause of the slightest regret among
Egyptians. Farouk eventually became a citizen of
the principality of Monaco, where he had available
to him the fortune he had foresightedly entrusted
to European banks. He spent the next 13 years in-
dulging his gross, extravagant tastes in the pleasure
spots of southern France, Italy and Switzerland
and died in March of 1965.

At the time of Farouk's overthrow it was several
weeks before the man really responsible for the
coup emerged to public view. He was the 34-year-
old Nasser, by then a lieutenant colonel, an instruc-
tor in military history and tactics at the War College. In appearance he was youthful and athletic
with wavy black hair and a prominent nose over a
clipped mustache. Although a man of sober mind
and little humor, he was to be portrayed in posters
as a dashing hero with a perpetually broad grin. He
reminded some of John Gilbert, the movie idol of

the nineteen-twenties. Others said he resembled a "Hitler of the Nile." Neither description was accurate.

Nasser, the son of a village postmaster transferred later to Alexandria, grew up in middle-class surroundings. On Government pay his family lived better than most Egyptians. He developed, however, a genuine affection for the peasants and just as genuine a hatred for their landlords, who considered the Nassers low class. It is interesting that after the 1952 revolution one of Nasser's first acts was to reform landholdings. Landowners were limited to 200 acres, and among the first estates to be broken up were those around Beni Mer, Nasser's village birthplace.

In his boyhood Nasser's rebel spirit often got him into trouble. He led school demonstrations against the British. When these spilled over into the streets of Alexandria he encountered policemen's clubs and today has a mark on his forehead to prove it. Yet he was a good student, interested in history, especially the history of liberation movements. He studied the American Revolution and became an admirer of George Washington, both as a military tactician and as "a man of peace."

However, Nasser, the conspirator and revolutionist, never studied what to do with a revolution once it had been won. Later he said the sole ambition of the 1952 revolutionaries had been to replace

Farouk with a government of honest, intelligent leaders from the military establishment and civilian life.

In his book, *Philosophy of the Revolution,* Nasser tells of his anguish when, the monarchy having been deposed, the magnitude of their task dawned upon him and his fellow officers.

"I thought we were only the pioneers and commandos," he wrote, "that we would be in the front for a few hours and that we would soon be followed by the solid masses marching to the goal."

He described the shock and disillusionment he experienced when it became clear that the men on whom the revolutionaries had counted for ideas— the university professors and the enlightened leaders of commerce and industry—would not rush in to support him. In fact, he complained, the very people from whom he expected help regarded the revolt only as "a weapon for revenge and hatred."

"I felt my heart charged with sorrow and dripping with bitterness," he continued. ". . . The mission of the vanguard had not ended. In fact, it was just beginning."

Land reform was the only immediate goal of Nasser's group. But before this was fairly well along, the Revolutionary Council ousted Naguib in favor of Nasser. Council members have said that Nasser had always been the real leader of the revolution, that Naguib was only a figurehead who not surprisingly tried to wield power when he found he enjoyed the role of front man. Nasser became Premier in 1954 and then President and has been the undisputed boss of Egypt ever since.

The lieutenant colonel who had never studied economics and knew nothing about foreign affairs soon realized that dispossession of big landlords and distribution of the expropriated land to peasants, while a step in the right direction, was insufficient to achieve his goals of social, political and economic reform.

There simply was not enough land for 26 million depressed people crowded into an arable area the size of Maryland. Nasser's agrarian reforms have distributed more than 600,000 acres among 125,000 formerly landless families comprising about 600,000 individuals. But this is equal to no more than the annual population increase in Egypt.

Nasser recognized early that he had to open faster roads to progress if he was to raise the standard of living for Egyptians, as he had always argued he could and would do were the corrupt king put aside. He decided the Aswan High Dam project offered the best solution to his problem.

For some time the British had considered the possibility of extending the use of the Nile's waters by building a new and higher dam at Aswan in Upper Egypt. Fifty years earlier they had built a low dam there with beneficial results. It had expanded the

farming area to the greatest limits known since ancient times—about six million acres.

But a new high dam—holding back more water
and allowing less to escape wastefully to the sea—
would enable Egypt to irrigate a million more acres
of desert land. Moreover, it would make it possible
to grow three crops a year on still another million
acres that produced only one crop annually. With
irrigation water Nile valley farmers can grow crops
the year around. Without irrigation they can plant
only a single crop after the river in flood has
brought its annual deposits of silt and moisture.

Once Nasser had fastened on the High Dam project as a way of easing his land problem he turned
to the United States and the International Bank for
Reconstruction and Development for loans.

He did this just when the late Secretary of State
John Foster Dulles was attempting to prod Egypt
into the anti-Communist bloc. Up to that time Nasser had not advanced his theories of neutralism, of
nonalignment with either the East or the West, and
was regarded by his own officers as so pro-Western
that many called him "Jimmy."

Nasser was doubtful about Dulles's prodding because it involved the British, whose troops were still
in Egypt, and the Turks, so recently in history the
tyrannical rulers of his country. Dulles wanted
Egypt and other Arab lands to join with Turkey
and Britain in the Baghdad Pact, described as a

defensive alliance against Communism.

While talks on the Aswan High Dam loan went ahead, Nasser resisted Dulles's Baghdad Pact plan. He did not confine his arguments to diplomatic channels but broadcast his growing convictions about neutralism and staying out of the East-West cold war over the Cairo radio's powerful "Voice of the Arabs."

The situation was further complicated by Nasser's claim that he needed modern armaments against Israel. He tried to buy these from the United States. When he was refused, out of American concern for Israel's safety, he obtained weapons from the Soviet Union through Czechoslovakia. This so enraged Secretary Dulles that he summarily canceled a tentative American offer of the Aswan loan. The World Bank and Britain, which had also discussed possible financial help for Nasser, followed suit and Nasser lost all hope of obtaining Western support for the dam. To add insult to injury in Nasser's view, Dulles said the United States had decided to withdraw its offer of aid because of Egypt's unstable condition.

In retaliation, revenge being an old Arab custom, Nasser nationalized the Suez Canal in a speech in Alexandria on July 26, 1956, the fourth anniversary of Farouk's abdication.

A chain reaction set in. Western powers, alarmed by the Nasser take-over of the British-dominated private Suez Canal Company and all this might mean to the vital oil traffic from the Middle East, began agitation that led to the Suez crisis of October and November, 1956. Israel, Britain and France invaded Egypt. The United Nations intervened with the unusual support of both the United States and the Soviet Union.

The invaders withdrew and the British-French plan to bring down Nasser left him stronger at home and across the Arab world.

Nasser tells his people and all Arabs every December 23, when he goes to Port Said to celebrate the final departure of the British troops, that the Egyptians successfully stood up against the "imperialist" invaders, that—and this is contrary to fact—they drove the enemy into the sea and back across the Sinai desert to Israel. He implies that he did in 1956 what Saladin did to the European intruders during the Crusades.

Never does he admit in these declamations that it was not Nasser or Egypt that settled the crisis but the United Nations in its peacekeeping role. Lester B. Pearson of Canada, acting for the world organization, worked out the peace formula in Cairo and subsequently won a Nobel Prize for it. To preserve the peace the United Nations established an Emergency Force on the Israeli-Egyptian border. It has stood there ever since.

With the departure of the foreign troops from

Egypt in 1956 Nasser could at last feel that his country was free of European domination. Thereafter he evolved his nonalignment policy, born perhaps at the 1955 conference of 29 African and Asian nations at Bandung, Indonesia, where Nasser for the first time emerged as a world figure. To Nasser neutralism or nonalignment means promising nothing to any of the major powers engaged in the cold war but standing ready to accept aid from all who offer it "without strings."

The Soviet Union after 1956 came to Nasser's aid not only with arms but also with Aswan Dam financing. It is committed to about 30 per cent of the $1 billion cost of the project, which is the largest public-works undertaking in either the Middle East or Africa. Both Moscow and Cairo want the dam to be a showpiece of progress through cooperation and "Socialist enterprise." Now half built, it is scheduled for completion by 1968, with the hydroelectric power station to be in full operation by 1970.

Meanwhile, although Nasser attacks Western "imperialism" without let-up, he receives equally important if less spectacular aid from the United States. Since the late nineteen-fifties, when Cairo's relations with Washington improved, Nasser has obtained $1 billion worth of American assistance, mostly in the form of wheat that Egyptians must have to maintain the standard of living Nasser has

promised them. Under the aid agreement Cairo
pays for the grain and other food not with dollars
but with Egyptian pounds and thus does not have
to expend "hard currency." Moreover, these Egyptian pounds are plowed back into the Egyptian
economy by the United States in the form of loans,
grants for exchange students and expenditures by
the American Embassy.

Were it not for this vital saving of "hard currency," Nasser would have long since exhausted the
loans and credits he has been given by East and
West to finance his ambitious development plans,
now in their second five-year stage. American dollars, British pounds sterling, West German marks
and certain other European currencies are known
as "hard" because they may be interchanged freely
in any country. Egyptian pounds are "soft" because they are not accepted, at least at face value,
in international money exchanges.

Nasser, piqued by American criticism of his
sending arms to the Congo rebels, declared at Port
Said in December, 1964, that "Egypt does not
need American food" because Egyptians would
rather tighten their belts than "sell their independence." Nevertheless, he and his economic aids
know they must count on buying United States
wheat with Egyptian pounds for another 10 to 15
years to survive.

The present fateful drive toward Nasser's revolutionary goals began with a series of drastic decrees in July, 1961. Landholdings were cut from a maximum of 200 acres to 100. Virtually all of Egypt's industry was placed under Government ownership or control. A ceiling of 5,000 Egyptian pounds ($14,150) a year was imposed on all salaries (except the President's, which is 6,000 Egyptian pounds). Other measures limited stockholdings and incomes and provided for profit-sharing by workers.

In an article for *The New York Times Magazine* of November 19, 1961, I wrote from Cairo: "This assault on class and privilege touched off the Syrian revolt [that dissolved the Syrian-Egyptian union, a subject I shall discuss in the next chapter]. Nasser's response has been to push harder at home. 'There is no longer room in Egypt for millionaires,' he told his people in a fighting speech. There has followed a wave of arrests and property seizures. . . .

"Nasser has staked his future on holding Egypt to his pattern of 'socialist, democratic, cooperative' society—with increasing emphasis on his brand of socialism."

It seemed to me at the time that he was encouraged to take this risk by the surprising success of the Egyptian management of the Suez Canal since 1956. When the waterway was nationalized the world freely predicted that the Egyptians would not be able to run it. But under Mahmud Younes,

Nasser's appointee, the Suez Canal Authority has done an outstanding job and today earns for the Government $160 million annually in "hard currency" from tolls charged ships transiting the canal.

How well has Nasser "liberated" his people? What has he done for the *fellaheen,* the Egyptian peasants? These questions are often put to correspondents in Cairo.

Nasser's own answer, when asked during an interview, was: "I have given them dignity."

I would say he has certainly made a start toward giving them dignity. But to give Egyptians full self-respect may be impossible during the lifetime of a single leader—even one who began as a dedicated young man.

As we have noted, Nasser has given some—but by no means a majority—of Egypt's landless peasants some farm land of their own. He has given Egyptians more work on the farms and in new factories, but there are still not enough really productive jobs to go around. He has given those of his countrymen who are employed higher incomes— 60 cents a day for common labor instead of the 28 cents that prevailed in King Farouk's time.

Nasser has provided television programs, with at least one TV set in each village center, and plenty of transistor radios. He has provided most large villages with a school, and Cairo University turns out more than enough teachers, although most are re-

luctant to leave Cairo for the backward villages. Socialized medicine has attacked the sight-impairing
trachoma and the debilitating bilharzia, improved
general health and cut the death rate from 22 per
1,000 in 1951 to less than 15 per 1,000 now.

Constantly exhorted to lift up his head,
straighten his shoulders and "stand afraid of no-
body," the Egyptian peasant in many ways is a
more "dignified" person than he was under past
overlords. But there is a misconception abroad
about Egyptians being restless for personal independence and impatient for Western-style democracy.

The long distance yet to go is apparent to any ob-
servant visitor. The prevailing thought in what
might be termed Egypt's body politic is still "Let
Gamal do it." And much as Gamal likes to talk
about the ouster of King Farouk in 1952, attribut-
ing it to a popular uprising of oppressed masses, the
Nasser revolution has still to penetrate to the roots
of Egyptian life.

Nasser, who calls himself a revolutionary and a
Socialist and thinks of himself as a populist, has not
yet been able to persuade his "liberated" people to
emerge from their 5,000 years of political lethargy,
nonresponsibility and nonenterprise. Observers in
Cairo are often amused, if that is the word, when
they hear it said on the outside that Nasser sup-
presses his masses.

For it is all too apparent that the Egyptian masses are far from eager to be rid of their pharaoh. Thus after six years in the Middle East I feel the role of Nasser's secret police is much overemphasized.

However, an active secret police does exist in the United Arab Republic. It is strong, but army intelligence watches over its shoulder lest it grow too powerful. In turn a corps of suprasecret police around Nasser maintains a constant vigil over the army. As an old army conspirator who made good, Nasser is aware that an army coup by a new crop of eager, ambitious, impatient "young officers" could take place again. Every few months rumors would spread through Cairo that high army echelons had been purged of suspected counterrevolutionaries.

One duty of the secret police is to keep Communists on a close leash. Nasser quickly abolished the Communist party, as he did all the old "reactionary" political parties of the prerevolutionary parliamentary government. He has authorized a succession of official political organizations, and since 1962 his one-party political structure has been based on his Arab Socialist Union.

Nasser never permitted his friendship with Communist governments—whether the Soviet Union, which is building the Aswan High Dam, or Communist China, with which he exchanges ambassadors

—to interfere with his suppression of Communists at home. In 1960 as many as 700 Communists and leftist sympathizers were held in desert detention camps. In the spring of 1964 all those remaining in custody—perhaps 250—were released by a Nasser decree. On the theory that they had "learned their lesson," as a Nasser aide put it, they were free to return to their homes and jobs.

The Egyptian press was nationalized in 1960 and is therefore under Nasser's strict control. Radio and television are owned by the state. The dispatches of foreign correspondents have been filed since 1962 without official censorship, but issues of newspapers carrying these dispatches frequently are not allowed into the country. Mail is often opened and telephones are periodically tapped. But control of speech, the press and other forms of expression is a phenomenon not of Egypt but of virtually all of the Middle East. The main difference, one suspects, is that Nasser's police do their job far less efficiently than do some others.

When Nasser became the ruler of Egypt he had no knowledge or experience whatsoever in foreign affairs. He had never been outside his own country. His view of the world was the limited one of a cadet and a lecturer on military history and science. Yet within a very few years he became an international figure whose fiery words have resounded in the world's major capitals. His lack of diplomatic experience and that of the other "young officers" he kept close about him should be remembered when we consider Nasser's relations with other world leaders.

VII

Nothing Works
the Way It Should

IN THE MIDDLE EAST, where at least one power—
Egypt—is trying to build rockets, locally made
matches may not strike nor locally manufactured
aspirin dissolve. In countries borrowing money to
build television transmitters the telephone exchange
has not yet been properly organized. Many con-
trivances do not function as they should.

This is true of politics and the apparatus of government. It is also true of international organizations established to weld the Middle East into a
unified force. The Arab League, the Baghdad Pact
(now the Central Treaty Organization), even the
Nasserist movement itself have never fulfilled their
basic purposes or worked as they were intended to.

The Arab League came into being in Cairo on

March 22, 1945. Leaders of seven Arab states signed a pact to work together for the common good. With the trouble with the Zionists in Palestine coming to a head, the Arabs felt an urgent need for a fresh start toward strength through unity. They formed their league with the help of the British.

That may seem strange since the British were abetting the Zionist cause, but Britain hoped to maintain her influence over the Arabs, who had grown restive about developments in Palestine, by supporting their aspirations for national identity, independence and racial unity. The British sought to control the Arabs through a loose federation.

The Arab League—or the League of Arab States, as it is officially called—proved to be a looser association than even the British could have hoped for. What the British didn't do to keep the league weak and ineffective, the Arabs did.

The original members of the league were Egypt, Saudi Arabia, Yemen, Jordan (then Transjordan), Iraq, Syria and Lebanon. They were joined later by the Sudan, Libya, Tunisia, Algeria, Morocco and Kuwait, giving the league a present membership of 13.

When the war with Israel broke out in 1948, it was widely expected that the young and vociferous Arab League would assert "the unity of the Arabs for the immediate destruction of Israel." To the surprise of all, except perhaps the Arabs themselves, this did not happen.

The league could not overcome a conflict of ideas and the jealousies of rival rulers. There was especially the dispute between the Hashemite rulers of Transjordan and Iraq and King Farouk of Egypt. In 1941, after the Vichy French surrender to the Nazis, Emir Abdullah, the Hashemite ruler of Transjordan, wanted to rush into Syria. He planned a Greater Syria, or a "Fertile Crescent," to unite the Arabs under the Hashemite crown. This alarmed the Egyptian and Saudi Arabian rulers and, more importantly, many Syrians. For in Syria a strong nationalist bloc had emerged to preserve the country's national integrity. Its leader, Shukri al-Kuwatli, was later, in 1958, to let Syria enter into a union with Nasser's Egypt.

As World War II neared its climax in late 1944, Emir Abdullah aroused suspicions among his Arab neighbors by fastening his sights on troubled Palestine. He spoke anew of uniting the Arabs. But other Arabs were sure that, whatever he said, he meant not "unity" but annexation of Palestine for himself. When the war over Palestine between the Arabs and the new state of Israel started, the Transjordanian Arab Legion, efficiently commanded and trained by British officers, was ready for action. Others, notably the Egyptians, were unready and also unwilling either to cooperate or to coordinate with the Transjordanians. The Arabs lost, as we have already noted, and the Arab League, far from "destroying Israel," barely managed to survive the strain of Arab dissension.

However, the Arabs were confident that once the British were gone, Arab nationalists could transform the league into a real power. The Nasser revolution of 1952 gave impetus to such expectations and Cairo seemed a promising center of operations. This great metropolis of the Arab Middle East had been for decades the center of most causes dear to Arab hearts. It seemed the logical place for a league secretariat, especially since Egyptian personnel and money would provide most of the backing. A handsome headquarters was constructed on the banks of the Nile where the British had built their barracks.

Egypt, the strongest and largest Arab country in point of population, had with Nasser's rise become the mecca of Arab nationalism. However, once the League's headquarters was established in Cairo, Egypt's very strength and Nasser's penchant for command made Moslem neighbors wary. So did the revolutionary aspirations of Arabs calling themselves Nasserites in countries from the Atlantic to the Persian Gulf.

There is hardly an Arab king or head of state who has not at one time or another either boycotted league councils or stayed away because he knew he would not be welcome. Iraq was ostracized after King Faisal II joined the pro-Western Baghdad Pact. King Saud of Saudi Arabia refused to attend meetings after Nasser accused him of an assassination plot. King Hussein of Jordan was for a long time *persona non grata* for "subservience" to Britain and the United States. President Habib Bourguiba of Tunisia would not come to Cairo three or four years ago because a man accused of trying to kill him had been given asylum by Nasser.

After his wave of Socialist decrees Nasser made no secret of the fact he, too, was "fed up" with the league. A confidant of the Egyptian President told me that the league "is a corpse."

"It represents only decadent kings and reactionary governments," he declared. "We [Nasserites] represent the revolutionary Arab people. There is a difference."

There were many months in 1962 and 1963 when a visit to the Arab League offices served correspondents little useful purpose. There was more logic in attending the annual receptions that marked the league's birthday. Refreshments were nonalcoholic, in keeping with Moslem custom. Still, attendance was worthwhile if only to see who came and, more interesting, who didn't.

Yet in January, 1964, President Nasser used the Arab League for an emergency Arab "summit" meeting—to devise countermeasures to Israel's imminent plan to divert waters of the Jordan River to irrigate the Negev desert. Astonishingly, 11 of the 13 heads of state attended in person and the other two were appropriately represented. The "reactionary" King Saud, who would be dethroned by his younger brother Faisal before many months, walked into the conference chamber arm-in-arm with Nasser, the "revolutionary." And President Bourguiba, emerging from his plane, was welcomed with one of Nasser's bear hugs—in effect an accolade.

The Arab rulers unanimously resolved to establish a unified military command, draw up a blueprint for Arab development of Jordan River water for Arab purposes and create a special fund, backed by contributions from all league members, to carry out the resolutions.

At this writing the unanimous resolutions are far from being put into force. But the rulers returned to Egypt six months later to discuss "progress." This time, in September, 1964, Nasser received them at Alexandria, on the Mediterranean, and entertained them in a style appropriate to late King Farouk's summering place.

It is often said that only the existence of Israel, which defeated them all in 1948 and successfully invaded Egypt in the 1956 Suez affair, has held the league's rival princes and revolutionaries together. But this is not wholly accurate. The league has become a rallying ground for liberating Arab lands from foreign interference. It has served as a platform for the causes of emancipation in the Sudan and Libya, Morocco and Algeria. The league is always ready to draft resolutions, although it is seldom able to act.

However, it has shown itself in a better light outside the political field. It has accomplished much in the way of cultural exchanges in and out of the Arab world. It has convened fruitful meetings of engineers, scientists and archeologists. It has promoted Arab interest and cooperation in civil aviation and communications. It works with the United Nations Educational, Scientific and Cultural Organization to preserve historical data. Recently its cultural committee completed a monumental and costly translation of Shakespeare into Arabic. Under Taha Hussein, a brilliant Egyptian scholar in his seventies, the committee has undertaken other massive projects to introduce Western literature to Arab readers.

The league has made notable starts at economic cooperation and has attempted the establishment of an Arab common market. It also maintains a boycott of Israel that some observers feel is more of a hindrance to Arab commerce than a handicap to the Israelis. But it has prevented Israel from using the Suez Canal.

* * *

In the nineteen-fifties Britain, with the full backing of the United States, proposed an alliance of all Middle Eastern powers to serve as a barrier to Soviet invasion or infiltration.

Turkey, under the late Premier Adnan Menderes, was the first to respond. Menderes, whose Democratic party had defeated in 1950 the People's Republican party founded by Ataturk, had adopted a strong pro-Western policy. Of course, Turkey, with Greece, had been a chief beneficiary of the United States under the Truman Doctrine of economic and military assistance. The Menderes Government was leaning for support ever more heavily on American aid.

Premier Menderes carried the burden of organizing the alliance, traveling anywhere any time he could obtain a receptive audience. He concluded a mutual assistance pact with Pakistan in 1954 and with Iraq in 1955, when Britain and Iran also formally joined what became known as the Baghdad Pact. The United States, while backing the pact from the start, has never joined it but has representatives on the pact's military and economic committees and also has mutual defense agreements with the alliance members.

To make it clear that the door to membership remained open to all the Arabs, the pact's headquarters and secretariat were established in the capital of Iraq, the only Arab member, and the organization was named for that city, Baghdad.

However, Nasser, already developing the policy of "positive neutralism" that he enunciated at the 1955 African-Asian conference in Bandung, spurned the Baghdad Pact. He berated it as one more attempt of the "imperialist" West to dominate the Middle East and he turned the powerful propaganda broadcasts of his "Voice of Cairo" against it.

Rumors that Jordan might join the alliance caused a crisis in Amman, the Jordanian capital, that nearly cost young King Hussein his throne. Iraq remained the pact's sole Arab member—but not for long.

Before the pact's second anniversary Iraq's membership became a factor in the overthrow of her pro-Western monarchy in the coup led by General Kassim, then a pro-Nasserist. The coup, in which King Faisal II and Premier Nuri as-Said lost their lives, took place on the eve of their scheduled departure for a meeting in Istanbul with other heads of Baghdad Pact states.

Iraq soon afterward withdrew from the pact. Thereupon its remaining members moved their headquarters from Baghdad to Ankara, where they renamed the alliance the Central Treaty Organization. It has had no contact with the Arabs since and the problem of coping with Communist infiltration in the Arab world has been left to the Arabs and their neutralist hero, Gamal Abdel Nasser.

* * *

Nasserism as an approach to Arab strength and self-sufficiency has not been able to evolve a lasting political entity outside Egypt, although it has made dramatic attempts. It is an element apart from the Arab League. It will have nothing to do with the Central Treaty Organization. No Nasser pact or agreement has worked for long. Yet Nasserism is a popular force that must be reckoned with in the affairs of the Middle East.

What is Nasserism? Reporting on Nasser's first decade in power, I wrote for *The New York Times Sunday Review* in July, 1962:

"The Revolution has been what Mr. Nasser says it is. It has been a 'search for dignity' for the wretched poor. It has been the avant garde of 'positive neutrality' in underdeveloped lands groping for confidence. Most recently, it has been the incubator of 'Arab Socialism,' aimed at hatching a new way of life not only for Egyptians but also for Arabs everywhere, for the Moslems and Africans."

Nasser disputes the claim of his detractors that he "thinks of Nasserism in terms of an Empire with him as Emperor." He has told visitors many times that "I do not seek to dictate to the Arab world," although he concedes that "Egypt's revolutionary experience may have equipped her for an important role in bringing about Arab unity."

However, Nasser somehow leaves the impression

with both his friends and his enemies, his ardent followers and his ambitious rivals, that the key to Nasserism—to social revolution in the Middle East—is clutched tightly in the hand of Gamal Abdel Nasser.

During the years I was in Cairo I often heard Nasser say that he wanted to lead Egyptians to a free and independent way of life that would continue after he had left the presidency. He told his ministers that he could not "indefinitely shoulder the burdens of high office." And in 1963 he inserted in a new constitution a provision for the election of a President for a new six-year term beginning in March, 1965.

Nasser then hinted that he might in 1965 retire in favor of another nominee. But a few weeks before the scheduled date for balloting, Nasser formally notified his one-party National Assembly of the approaching election. There were immediate "demands" from all parts of the Arab world that he continue in office. The controlled Cairo press reported that "one million Egyptians" had poured into the capital from the villages to demonstrate for the nomination of Nasser. The demonstrations kept the city in a holiday-like state for nearly 10 days, and when the time came the National Assembly voted "unanimously" for the nomination of *El Rais,* the Leader. There were no other nominations. Responding to the acclaim, Nasser said: "I had

hoped to give up this office at this time. But, perhaps, you are right." He agreed to run in the un-
contested election. It was held March 15, 1965, and
he received 99.999 per cent of the votes. And in
Egypt the people turn out to vote, for a male Egyptian who neglects to do so is subject to a fine he cannot afford.

There have now been at least a half-dozen attempts to transfer Nasser's popularity at home and
abroad into mergers, federations or alliances of
Arab states. The first and most dramatic was the
merger of Egypt and Syria to form the United Arab
Republic on February 22, 1958.

After the British-French-Israeli attack on Egypt
in 1956 had discredited the West in Arab eyes, the
Soviet Union made new efforts to get a Communist hold on the Middle East. The Communists had
found Nasser's Egypt tough to infiltrate. Hundreds
of them were jailed in the early years of the revolution and the Communist party was outlawed along
with all other political organizations. The Soviet
Union, therefore, directed its principal drive
against Syria.

Syria was unstable and had undergone a series of
government turnovers. Moscow offered to help
"stabilize" administrative and other affairs with
weapons, economic aid and technical assistance.
Several Communists worked their way into high
office. The Socialists and Nasserists were split.

It appeared to Syrian supporters of Nasser, and perhaps to Nasser himself, that the shaky Government of Shukri al-Kuwati might fall entirely into the clutches of Moscow. Among the Nasserists in Damascus, the Syrian capital, was one who decided to act. He was Colonel Abdel Hamid Serraj, a young, able and unscrupulous chief of the Syrian Deuxieme Bureau (Intelligence). He had managed to put the pro-Egyptian element of the Syrian Army in key posts, his efforts being made easier by the fact that Nasser at the time was nearing the peak of his prestige.

Carefully timing his design, Colonel Serraj boldly jailed important Communist leaders and persuaded the aging and weary Kuwatli to give up his difficult office. Then Serraj went to Nasser with a proposal of union between Syria and Egypt.

Nasser responded in a remarkably short time— he has since conceded that he acted "too quickly— we were not ready for union." He signed a merger agreement with Serraj and the two countries were joined as The United Arab Republic. Nasser appointed Serraj to the security post of Minister of Interior for Syria and made Field Marshal Abdel Hakim Amer, his Egyptian Vice President and closest friend, his personal representative in Damascus.

The Arab world was electrified. In Lebanon civil war broke out in the spring and only the landing of marines from the United States Sixth Fleet prevented victory for Nasser-supported opponents of pro-Western President Camille Chamoun. King Hussein of Jordan had to ask for British paratroopers to save him from the threat of overthrow by army coup. In July, as we have noted, pro-Nasserist forces in Iraq led by Kassim brought down the Iraqi monarchy. Nasser seemed then on top of the Arab world.

But he soon found out that popularity does not immediately mean power. Many Arab nationalists in Syria, Iraq, Jordan and Lebanon who had proclaimed Nasser their champion and hero came to realize that they did not want to work under him or obey his commands. Also, in the next two years Nasser was to discover how different Egyptians were from Syrians, despite their common language and religion.

The Egyptian peasant is a settled man, used to farming in one spot and working under one master perhaps for a lifetime. The Syrian is by tradition a mobile tribesman. He owes allegiance to community chiefs rather than to national leaders and certainly not to a foreign master. Egypt is a country that has known wealth confined to a few families. Syria has always had multitudes of merchants and small businessmen, Levantine traders long in contact with the commerce of the Mediterranean world. Their hobby is political intrigue.

Confident of his popularity, manifested in tre-

mendous street ovations every time he toured the
Syrian portion of the United Arab Republic, Nasser
moved boldly into the Socialist phase of his revolution in the summer of 1961. His decrees nationalizing, sequestrating and confiscating millions of
dollars' worth of property for the Government ap-
plied to Syria as well as to Egypt. The "Arab Socialist" decrees were accepted without an audible mur-
mur in Cairo, where it was taken for granted that
"something must be done" to raise the peasants'
standard of living. But in Damascus there was
great hullabaloo. Merchants, importers, bankers
screamed their protest at losing their property and
lifetime earnings. Syrian politicians complained that
Nasser had not bothered to consult them before is-
suing his drastic decrees, something no Egyptian
would have thought of complaining about.

When Nasser, in a final command, directed the
Syrian Cabinet to leave Damascus and live hence-
forth in Cairo, even Colonel Serraj resigned. In a
quick painless army coup Syria seceded and the
United Arab Republic broke up. Nasser decreed
that the name be retained, though today it applies
only to Egypt.

We have dealt in this chapter with three approaches to unity in the Middle East. All have
failed.

The Arab League is virtually impotent without

the intermittent infusion of Nasser's dynamic personality. The league's secretary general, Abdel Khaled Houssana, is a hard-working, well-meaning, discreet Egyptian diplomat who is known to very few Arabs outside his secretariat in Cairo.

The Baghdad Pact aspired to unify the Middle East, including the Arabs, but hopes were dashed when Nasser, for reasons of his own, induced the Arabs to stand clear of military alliances.

Nasser, because of his dramatic successes and the political stamina he has shown in Egypt, remains the outstanding voice of Arab unity. But he has failed to build a house strong enough, and yet sufficiently decompartmentalized, to keep all the relatives happy together. Crowds that shout outdoors for Nasser have shrunk from living in Nasser's house, even though he has from time to time altered the design of Nasserism to please the tenants. However much Nasser's dynamism may alarm the West, it sometimes frightens the Middle East more and certainly has not yet united it.

No scheme for Middle East unity, among the Arabs or anyone else, has considered a role for Israel except as this "unwanted" state may be used to drive Arabs together.

This has not been enough.

VIII

Arabs versus Communism

WHEN THE ARABS spurned Western alliance they may have seemed to leave the door open for Communist infiltration. Nasser's acceptance since the late nineteen-fifties of Soviet arms and massive aid to build the Aswan High Dam has appeared to outsiders to constitute an invitation to Communists to enter Egypt and, through Egypt, the rest of the Middle East and the whole of Africa. But Communist plans to subvert the Middle Eastern kings and other rulers or the Arab nationalists have not worked out any better than the Arabs' unity schemes. Communists are held in jail in Iraq, Jordan and Saudi Arabia and until recently were jailed in the United Arab Republic and Algeria.

Nevertheless there is continuing Communist interest in the Middle East. Indeed, the Soviet Union and Communist China are contesting each other for paramount influence there. In Africa Chou En-lai, the Chinese Premier, has made some inroads lately, but he has little appeal for the Arabs, the Turks or the Iranians. Nikita S. Khrushchev, when he was the Soviet leader, did better, but undoubtedly his gregarious personality had something to do with it.

I saw both Chou and Khrushchev when they came to Cairo only a few months apart in late 1963 and early 1964. The Chinese Premier inspired no warmth whatever. Official coolness was probably responsible, for President Nasser was not about to embarrass the Soviet Union, his partner in building the dam that will be his monument.

However, in May, 1964, when Khrushchev became the first Soviet ruler to set foot on Middle Eastern or African soil, his overwhelming reception was more than an official gesture. As he stepped ashore in Alexandria, Egyptians wearing long flowing gowns broke through security cordons to touch him. During the welcoming parade in Cairo a young girl ecstatically threw herself across the hood of his car. Khrushchev, though taken aback by the casual security that allowed such unrestrained behavior, responded as only he could—with that great toothy grin, arms flying wide open, waving his straw hat until the Egyptian sun, burning his bald head, forced him to put it back on.

At the beginning Khrushchev hailed Nasser as an ideological brother. In an address before the National Assembly in Cairo Khrushchev said: "We [as Marxists] accept your Arab Socialism. We are working for the same ends. We hail your leader, Nasser."

Nasser beamed at the accolade although he had opposed Communism ever since coming to power and had been tough on Communists and fellow-travelers. He had released several hundred of them from desert detention camps just a few weeks before Khrushchev's arrival, but whether this was a timely gesture toward the Soviet Union was never made clear. In any event the Egyptian Communist party had long since ceased to exist as a political force, Nasser's Arab Socialist Union being the only official political grouping.

Doctrinaire Communists have never thought much of Nasser's "Socialist philosophy," although, like Khrushchev, they have from time to time praised it as a "new phenomenon in the Arab world" and, as such, a step in the right direction. It may be a "step," but Nasser's Arab Socialism is, in fact, a mixture of ideologies. It is Socialist when it calls for public ownership of heavy industry, transportation and communications. It is capitalist when it insists on private ownership of land. Nasser has found no place for the collective farm so dear to the heart of Communists—and even Israeli Socialists.

The land taken from the landlords has been given with a deed and for a cash payment to landless peasants. Arab Socialism is certainly non-Marxist when it builds on the religious foundation of Islam. Marxist Socialism is based on a materialist philosophy and admits the existence of no God.

Perhaps the religious difference alone can keep Communism out of the Middle East in the long run. Khrushchev may have got some notion of this barrier during his historic visit to the United Arab Republic. The Imams' long chanted prayer—always harsh to non-Moslem ears—that is ritual at the opening of any public meeting visibly annoyed Khrushchev. Nasser, a devout if hardly fanatic Moslem, included prayers in the ceremony marking the completion of the first stage of the Aswan dam. Khrushchev, the honor guest, told aides he thought that out of respect for him, an atheist, Nasser should have dispensed with the religious preliminary. But for Moslems this would have been impossible.

Before his two-week sojourn was over, Khrushchev showed irritation about another aspect of Arab Socialism. At Aswan he heard interminable speeches in which, it seemed to him, Nasser and his guests—President Abdel Salam Arif of Iraq and President Abdullah al-Salal of Yemen—spoke of Arab Socialism with more emphasis on "Arab" than on "Socialism."

"Socialism," he lectured the Arab leaders in a later speech, "is for workers everywhere. It is not only for Arabs, or for Russians. I am a Socialist first and a Russian second. In Russia we are not Russian Socialists—we have 110 nationalities among us. . . ."

Arabs, he declared, should be less nationalist and more worker-minded if they want full admission to the world brotherhood of Socialism.

Such long-run obstacles in the Middle East do not, of course, deter Communists from driving for immediate goals and quick victories over the Western world.

Communists, in the Soviet Union, China or wherever, are already enjoying the negative benefits of Nasser's neutralism and nonalignment. For not only has Nasser spurned Western anti-Communist alliances (while accepting Western aid); he has also refrained from attacking Communist countries in his speeches and Cairo's propaganda broadcasts. When asked during an interview why as a neutralist he never found occasion to criticize Moscow or Peking, Nasser quickly replied: "We never attack anyone. We only counterattack. When the West attacks us, we answer. We answer the East, too, when they attack, but they seldom do. And remember, it has been the Western imperialists who have always invaded us, never the Communists."

But Communists do not invade, they infiltrate, and they may yet slip in through Egypt's back door. Southern Egypt adjoins the Sudan, where after rioting in November, 1964, a Government was installed with four Communists in the 15-member Cabinet.

The Sudan is a predominantly Negro country whose northern area alone is Moslem. The northern Sudanese have a mixture of Egyptian and Arab blood and have long had an intimate relationship with the people of Upper Egypt, as southern Egypt is called.

It is through the Sudan that Nasser has been shipping military aid to the Congolese rebelling against Premier Moise Tshombe's Government. Nasser's hatred of Tshombe—he regards the Congolese Premier as an "imperialist stooge"—has blinded him to the significance of the rebels' adherence to Communist China. Conceivably Nasser could find Communist influence coming into southern Egypt through the Sudan, his very pipeline to the Congo.

We have noted before how Syrians endured a series of weak regimes after World War II that played into the hands of the Communists. Syria, in fact, produced one of the leading Communist organizers in the Middle East, Khalid Bakdash. In 1958 the alarmed merchants and traders backed union with Nasser's Egypt to save themselves from the Communist "plotters" who wanted to destroy their free enterprise. Nasser took Syria under his wing, but when he disclosed his own designs for a Government take-over of private business the Syrians broke away. To them Nasserism then seemed the fate worse than death.

During the Egyptian-Syrian merger Bakdash the Communist was exiled. Since then he has not been able to re-establish himself with Syria's ruling Baath (Arab Renaissance) party. The Baath movement was founded by revolutionary intellectuals led by Michel Aflak. While Aflak shared many of Nasser's social objectives, his influence declined during the merger, but it survived in the parliament that followed Syria's secession from Egypt. His party then came to power in a coup d'état of March, 1963. The Baath, in principle democratic, has since resorted to dictatorial methods to suppress its opponents, whether rightists or leftists, whether Nasserists, Communists or merchant traders.

The Syrian-Egyptian merger undoubtedly encouraged Iraqi nationalists to stage the 1958 coup that overthrew the monarchy and took Baghdad out of the Baghdad Pact. The accession to power of Abdul Karim Kassim was a gain for the Nasserists and a blow to the Communists until Kassim decided to use the Communists to keep the Nasserists from overwhelming him. Gradually, as Kassim executed scores of Nasserists and threw hundreds of them in jail, he fell more and more into the hands of the

Communists. But Communist plans were overtaken by a Baathist-Nasserist coup in January, 1963, and Kassim was executed.

The coup brought to power Abdel Salam Arif, who, assuming the presidency, has pursued an anti-Communist policy at home while aligning himself with Nasser and emulating the Egyptian leader to the point of wooing Moscow for the sake of arms and economic aid.

A tripartite Arab Socialist union of the United Arab Republic, Syria and Iraq (to be called the United Arab Republic) was agreed upon in Cairo in April, 1963. But this most ambitious of recent efforts at unity did not survive preliminary stages. Without fear, for the moment, of a Communist threat, the Syrian Baathists could not face a second time the prospect of Nasser domination and possible destruction of their organization.

However, Arif, who did have a Communist problem, joined hands with Nasser in a federation designed eventually to unite Iraq and Egypt. For various reasons, including the fact the two countries are so far apart geographically, this association has not progressed beyond planning for cultural exchanges and mutual military defense. But it has had one effect—that of helping Arif stabilize his weak Government against Communist infiltration.

In Turkey and Iran, non-Arab nations that by

their adherence to the Central Treaty Organization
avow Western alignment, Communism has no active being. Both countries maintain diplomatic ties,
as do the Arabs, with the Soviet Union, and the relationship varies from cool to cordial. Both countries are deeply indebted to the West and to American economic and military aid, without which they
would have been torn apart by internal political
strains abetted, no doubt, by the Communists.

The reaction that has set in is natural and perhaps inevitable. In both Turkey and Iran resentment against the United States is growing, especially among students, university faculties and, one
hesitates to say it, journalists. From them I have
heard over and over the charge that United States
aid supports not the people but the government or
party in power.

One reason for this resentment is that Turkey
and Iran, like many debtors, don't love their chief
creditor. Because of extensive borrowing from the
West, including several European countries as well
as the United States, Turkey in 1965 alone must
pay $215 million in interest on foreign loans. This
debt, educated Turks realize, complicates tremen-
dously the financing of their country's five-year development plan, which must be carried out, on top
of all the previous development work, to assure
modest prosperity and progress.

The resentment against benefactors has nurtured

in both Turkey and Iran a "neutralist" trend. Neither Turks nor Iranians seem able to abide Nasser,
but many of them rather like the way he gets help
from both East and West and retains the privilege
of thumbing his nose at anyone who irritates him.
These Turks and Iranians, while they would not
think of doing it themselves, half admire someone
who tells the United States to "go jump in the lake,"
as Nasser did in his Port Said speech in December, 1964.

Neither Turkey nor Iran is likely in the foresee-
able future to go "neutralist" or break her ties with
the Central Treaty Organization or, in the case of
Turkey, a NATO member, the North Atlantic
Treaty Organization. But both may try Nasser's experiment of doing business with Communist Russia
and other Eastern-bloc countries while suppressing
Communists.

Russia and Turkey have now exchanged visits by
legislative groups, and in the fall of 1964 the first
visit by a Turkish Foreign Minister to the Soviet
Union in 25 years took place. These events were attended by speculation that Turkey and Russia
might at last be ending their ancient feud.

Two facts lend credence to this possibility. First,
the Soviet Union, more than Britain or the United
States, has seemed to favor the maintenance of an
independent Cyprus. While Turks despise the
Greek-dominated Cyprus Government of Arch-

bishop Makarios, they would rather have it than
enosis—the union of Cyprus and Greece. The
Turks feel let down by the West, particularly by
the United States, for its failure to support whole-
heartedly the Turkish stand on Cyprus. The Soviet
Union in a way is more pro-Turkish than Turkey's
Western allies.

Second and even more important, Moscow, un-
less new leaders and new policies intervene, is ready
to become a new long-term creditor of Turkey.
This is what Turkey needs to get on with her ambitious development program, which includes the
vast Keban Dam project on the upper Euphrates
River in the eastern part of the country. It would
cost about $350 million. Turkey cannot finance this
dam by itself, but a number of Western nations, including the United States, have now moved to frus-
trate any Soviet plans to do for Turkey what Russia
did for Egypt at Aswan.

The United States announced in July, 1965, it
will lend Turkey $40 million to help meet the for-
eign exchange costs of the Keban power project. The
rest of the needed $135 million in foreign currency
will come from West Germany, France, Italy, the
European Investment Bank and the International
Development Association.

Events of 1964 and 1965 seem to indicate a
communist trend toward alliance, through Nasser,

with the Arabs. We see increasing rivalry between the Soviet Union and Red China to court the Arabs. They do it not only with aid and promises of aid but also with moral support in the dispute with Israel over use of the Jordan River waters.

As the Communists openly woo the Arabs, the middle-course position of the United States in the Middle East becomes more difficult. Both former Premier Khrushchev and Premier Chou en-Lai paid personal visits to Cairo in 1964. But no high-ranking United States official has been there since Secretary of State Dulles went to plead (in vain) for Nasser's support of the Baghdad Pact in the early nineteen-fifties. And certainly no English or French minister of equal rank has been there since 1956. No United States official ever speaks out for support of the Arabs as the Russian and Red Chinese leaders now do. American aid, while considerable, goes to the Arabs in the "interests of Middle East stability," rather than in support of their cause. On the contrary, United States officials, from the President down, find frequent occasions on which to pledge support to the state of Israel.

So an East-West division may be in the making. If a war should erupt over the Jordan River dispute (to be discussed in a later chapter), Nasser is confident the United States would soon find a way to send its Mediterranean (Sixth) Fleet to the relief of Israel. Up to the present he has not been sure

that the Soviet Union would support him with anything more than the planes, tanks and guns already in Egypt. But the Soviet Union in the future
might want to demonstrate to the Arabs that it,
and not Communist China, is the Arab socialists'
big brother. The state of the East-West cold war in
places as far distant as Vietnam and Berlin could
forestall such a step. Yet the Kremlin might decide
the time was just right for all good Communists to
stand up and be counted on the side of Arab brothers fighting "imperialism."

IX

The Kings Grow Wary

WHEN NASSER CAME to power he eliminated one of the richest and oldest monarchies in the Middle East, the century-and-a-half-old Alid dynasty of King Farouk. It is only natural that the fall of such a monarch as Farouk caused other Middle Eastern kings to view with alarm this revolutionary interloper. Some were leaders, or descendants of leaders, who had helped Britain and France put an end to Turkish domination in 1917–18. They later were sponsored by the Western powers as rulers of what then amounted to colonial domains.

In the early years of Nasser's revolution the Kings of Saudi Arabia, Jordan and Iraq and other crowned heads saw Nasser as a brash upstart who would soon undo himself. But every knockdown

became a boost. When the British, French and Israelis tried to take the nationalized Suez Canal
away from Nasser in 1956, the United Nations,
with the combined support of the United States and
the Soviet Union, pulled them back. The canal remained in Nasser's hands. When Washington refused to sell Nasser arms and to help finance the
Aswan High Dam, he got what he wanted from
Moscow.

After 1956 it was clear to those who wished him
the worst that Nasser was in power to stay. He was
enjoying surprising success in gaining the ears of
royal subjects in many Arab lands and was on the
way to becoming their hero.

More was to come. In 1958 the republic of Syria
joined Egypt, and the King of Iraq fell in what was
then a pro-Nasserist coup. In 1961 Nasser's Socialist
decrees and the Cairo radio's stepped-up attacks on
"corrupt, reactionary despots" truly alarmed the
kings. To Hussein of Jordan, Saud of Saudi Arabia
and the medieval-minded Imam of Yemen the Syrian breakaway in September, 1961, seemed an
omen of hope.

To Nasser's fury, Jordan, Saudi Arabia, and Turkey as well, recognized the newly independent
Syria within a day or two after her secession from
the United Arab Republic. Egypt severed relations with all three.

The senile Imam of Yemen composed from his

sick bed a poem denouncing Nasser's Socialism as anti-Islamic. Nasser abruptly terminated the curious Federation of Arab States that for two or three years had associated politically the feudal Yemeni Imamate with the revolutionary United Arab Republic.

While the Imam's poem was the subject of many derisive cartoons in the Cairo press, it did much in the end to disrupt Arab unity. For the poem and the Egyptian-Yemeni break inspired a pro-Nasserist army plot that sparked a revolution in the last country in the Arab world where anyone, including Nasser, had expected a revolt. That country was Yemen.

The old Imam died in September, 1962. Within 10 days his son, Imam Mohamad al-Badr, who ironically was moderately progressive and had once been on good terms with Nasser, was overthrown. The leader of the army coup, Abdullah al-Salal, backed by little more than a palace guard, immediately asked Nasser for help. While he held the two main cities—Sana, the capital, and Taiz—Salal needed armed forces to subdue unruly tribesmen whom the old Imam had kept in line by holding hostages in a Taiz prison. Salal himself had been chained in a cell for seven years.

To the surprise of Salal and almost everyone else, Nasser responded with a large and costly expeditionary force. Just why he did so still remains a mystery.

Yemen was 1,000 miles away from Egypt. Few
Egyptians knew exactly where it was. Only a hand-
ful had ever been there. Egyptians had been told
that some day they might have to fight Israel, but it
had never occurred to any of them that they would
be sent to a foreign land to fight other Arabs. After
all, to prevent "the killing of Arab brothers," Nasser had said not too many months before that he
had decided against landing troops in Syria to prevent the 1961 secession.

Nasser has denied when asked about it that the
Yemeni revolution was of his making. He told a
correspondent that he had no advance warning of
the coup and simply found the news on his desk one
morning.

But he received the news "happily" because revolution in the isolated country, once known as Arabia Felix (Happy Arabia), was long overdue. Con-
ditions in Yemen were 1,000 years out of date.
There had not been a yard of paved road in the
country until the Chinese Communists, for some
reason known only to the late Imam, were granted
permission to build such a road from Hodeida on
the Red Sea to Sana a few years ago. The Americans
were building another from the seacoast to Taiz
and on to Sana at the time of the revolution.

Nasser said it took him 12 days to make up his
mind on the unusual course of armed intervention
in Yemen. He committed the Egyptian forces with

the explanation that "we were asked for help, and
we will remain there until it is certain the revolution is secure."

It was the consensus of diplomatic opinion in
Cairo that Nasser felt that by sending troops he
would demonstrate to Arabs everywhere that
Egypt's strength was available "in a good cause"
whenever called upon. But certainly Nasser did not
think the demonstration would last so long and tie
down so many troops and so much equipment. As
this is written, 34 months after the revolution took
place, the Salal Government has declared "victory"
many times—but about 50,000 of Nasser's troops
are still in Yemen to "secure" this "victory."

Nasser miscalculated in not realizing that the
5,000,000 Yemeni were less conscious of revolutionary causes, of Arab unity and perhaps of Arab
nationalist heroes than they were of tribal powers
and privileges. By linking his revolution with one
Moslem sect and certain tribes in the cities of Sana
and Taiz, Abdullah al-Salal automatically alien-
ated a whole set of tribal enemies inhabiting the
plain and mountain country of the north and east.
The ousted Imam found shelter among friendly
tribes without difficulty and began operating from
a mountain cave near the Saudi Arabian border. His
runners, slipping in and out of Sana at will,
brought him word of Egyptian positions, and with
a walkie-talkie he gave orders for guerrilla attack.

Egyptian tanks bogged in the sand and were blown up. Egyptian patrols were ambushed and killed. Yemeni warriors seldom bothered to take prisoners. And the Egyptian bomber pilots found few worthwhile targets.

The trackless wastes of Yemen have proved a costly training ground for the Egyptians, for all their Soviet equipment. Even the elite desert commandos, always the hit of the Revolution Day Parade in Cairo, have not proved effective against the Yemeni hillmen.

The Imam has not made good his promise to lead his guerrilla royalists back to Sana. But no one expected him to be holding out in a cave inside Yemen nearly three years after he was forced out of his capital.

The shrewd Faisal of Saudi Arabia is the principal cause of the Imam's ability to hold out. For the civil war in Yemen has given Faisal, who since the outbreak has succeeded his older brother Saud as King, an easy and cheap way to embarrass his rival, Nasser, and reduce his image as the great Arab nationalist hero. All Faisal has had to do is slyly pass just enough arms and ammunition over to the Imam's royalists to keep Salal worried and Nasser's forces tied down.

Faisal and Nasser are interesting rivals because they are so well matched in cunning. One feels each enjoys this Arab gamesmanship too much to take seriously efforts by the United States and other powers to disengage them and end the Yemen war through compromise.

Faisal and Nasser had been old friends, and even when they met in September, 1964, for the Arab summit conference in Alexandria, they visited easily and in fact agreed to a disengagement including the withdrawal of Egyptian forces.

King Faisal has said he always found Cairo a cultural center of gravity and came to think of Nasser as a man he could not help admiring, even though he realized that Nasser represented forces committed to destroying Faisal's family and kingdom. Before the Yemeni hostilities Faisal, as Crown Prince and then Premier, was friendly with Nasser. He tried, he has said, to get along with him "as far as possible." In the early years of the Egyptian revolution Faisal was considered anti-American and pro-Nasser. He made large real-estate investments in Cairo and maintained a palatial residence there. He built—and owned until Nasser nationalized it—a 30-story apartment tower, the tallest building in Cairo. He defended Nasser's seizure of the Suez Canal in 1956—but Nasser's "seizure" of Yemen, as Faisal saw it, was quite another matter.

Over and above personal rivalry, Faisal and Hussein believed that Nasser was using the Yemeni revolt—if, indeed, he had not provoked it—as a pretext for gaining a foothold in the oil-rich Arabian

peninsula. The monarchs, and Britain as well, have
not been satisfied with Nasser's firm denials. London thinks Nasser plainly has been moving into
southern Arabia both to get at oil and to have a
base from which to drive the British out of their
colony of Aden and the sheikdoms of the British-
protected South Arabian Federation. Britain accordingly has never recognized the Salal regime, although the United States did so, and has tried to use
this as a lever to pry Egypt and Saudi Arabia apart
in Yemen. At this writing each of these outside antagonists, while professing strong desires to withdraw, waits for the other to make the first step
backward.

The Egyptians say their troops are not only
fighting royalist "rebels" but also helping Yeminis
build and train an army, a government and a civil
service. There can be no doubt that there is plenty
for foreign "advisers" to do in Yemen. At the time
of the Salal coup there were not enough educated
men and technicians in Yemen to cope with a national administration. For example, there was only
one qualified pilot; he was appointed Minister of
Aviation. The Yemeni Airlines, consisting of three
American-built two-motor planes, was of course
taken over by the arriving Egyptian "advisers."

There can be no doubt that without Nasser's
technicians and at least a small expeditionary force,
the revolution there could not have lasted 30 days,

and it is possible that Yemen would have lost her opportunity to emerge into the 20th century.

When I visited Yemen in October, 1962, one month after the revolution, the Yemenis were seeing their first foreign journalists. The old Imam had not admitted newspapermen except in rare instances on his personal invitation when they would be his guests. Salal, feeling his revolutionists had served a cause of "liberation" worthy of world acclaim, opened the borders to all correspondents.

Among the first to arrive, I was escorted for room and board to the late Imam's guest house, now operated by the Foreign Ministry. There was no hotel or restaurant in all of Yemen, no newsstand or movie theater.

I found Yemeni men walking the dusty streets with a rifle over the shoulder and a crescent-shaped dagger at the belt. The guns and knives were status symbols rather than weapons. I found it comforting to see the rifle barrels usually plugged with cotton to protect them from the dust. These town dwellers were the kindest, friendliest, simplest people I met in the Middle East.

The only money the Yemenis knew were 18th-century Austrian coins, silver Maria Theresa thalers handed out by the Imam to the deserving and loyal and declared invalid as legal tender by the Salal regime as of May 1, 1965. The only national treasury was the vault in the Imam's palace. When he died the location of some of his caches remained a mystery for weeks and months.

"We do not know how much money we have," complained Abdullah al-Salal. "The Imam kept no books. There is no Government budget. There has not been one for 1,000 years."

Salal said Yemen needed not only military help to save his revolution but also civil administrators, fiscal experts, teachers, engineers, doctors "and almost any kind of technical assistance you can imagine." He asked Nasser for help, he said, "because we knew he was our friend and would aid us all he could."

Although he has not made his peace with them, Nasser insists he has no ambition to remove all kings and sheiks. Accused once of such a goal, he replied: "That is quite untrue. We have no objection to monarchies as such. We have most friendly relations with the Kings of Morocco, Libya and Kuwait." He said he opposed only kings who showed no regard for their peoples and wasted their revenues "building palaces."

But after the experience in Yemen the remaining Arab monarchs are weary. Only Israel can rally the dissenting kings and Socialist heads of state. Israel's plan to divert Jordan River water for her own purposes accomplished this in 1964—but to what if any lasting result remains to be seen.

The man most concerned, King Hussein of Jor-

dan, where irrigated lands are most affected by the
Israeli plan, worked arduously at the Arab summit
meetings in Egypt to get right and left in the Arab
world together. He unquestionably had some impact then. But how effective this English-trained
young man can be only Allah knows.

The vital importance of that water to the coun-
tries involved, to the Middle East and perhaps to
Arab unity and the final settlement of the Arab-
Israeli dispute will be discussed in the next chapter.

X

The Middle East Runs on Water

CONTRARY TO POPULAR BELIEF, the Middle East does not live on oil but on water. For lack of enough water millions exist at subsistence levels.

"My people cannot drink oil," Nasser has said, explaining that Egypt's fundamental need is not the Middle East's petroleum fields but cheap water to irrigate the 97 per cent of his country too arid to farm.

The Shah of Iran told me once that with enough dams and wells—water wells, not oil wells—Iran could support three times her present population of 22 million at a European standard of living. This is something Iran's rich petroleum fields have not enabled the country to do.

The whole Middle East is short of rainfall except for narrow strips along the Mediterranean Sea.

From its banks almost anywhere along its 4,000-mile course the Nile is beautiful. It is not Nile green but usually muddy brown. Yet it is beautiful because it brings to life every inch of soil it touches. In fact, it does more. Every foot of arable land in Egypt has been built up through the centuries by the accumulation of silt brought down by the Nile in flood. So the ancients always said "Egypt is the gift of the Nile." More exactly, it is the gift of Ethiopia, Uganda and other Central African highlands whence came the water and rich soil deposits.

Egypt does not contribute one drop to the Nile. On the ground the great river is as broad as the Mississippi. But from the air it is but a serpent slithering through a patchwork of green fields— a narrow patchwork except at the Nile Delta, a patchwork surrounded by brown and barren desert stretching to the horizon.

North and East of Egypt are the Tigris and the Euphrates rivers, in whose now-arid valleys once flourished ancient Sumer, Babylonia, Assyria and Persia. Smaller than the Nile, the Tigris or the Euphrates is the Jordan River, but along its banks grew up the great faiths of the Jew, the Christian and the Moslem.

These rivers that nourished civilizations from the

beginning of recorded time wander today, aimlessly it seems, through long stretches of wasteland. In Turkey I have traveled all day along the bounding freshet that so buoyantly carries the melted snows off the rugged Anatolian mountains, but from a plane the Euphrates is seen forcing its way down a bleak, often forbidding course.

Too little has been done to develop these water basins because in the Middle East public works and reclamation always get involved detrimentally in foreign policy and international intrigue. In comparison the seemingly endless disputes among American states when it comes to dividing the waters, say, of the Colorado River are as nothing. And the Jordan River, for special reasons we shall note, presents problems of supercomplexity.

The building of the Aswan High Dam in Upper Egypt, whose history we have already related, is a classic example of the ramifications of Middle Eastern development schemes. Nasser's decision that the dam be built led, as we have seen, to the nationalization of the Suez Canal and the worst crisis the Middle East had experienced since the creation of Israel. It had much to do with the shaping of Nasser's policy of nonalignment, for it taught him that he could not depend altogether on the West and probably should not depend on either the West or the East alone for all the help he would need to modernize Egypt.

Compared with the Suez Canal crisis, Egypt's differences with other Nile River countries over the dam seem minor. But agreements had to be negotiated, especially with the Sudan, where lands and the whole city of Wadi Halfa would be flooded by the dam's waters. The Sudan finally accepted 15 million pounds (about $35 million) as compensation for the loss of land and the cost of moving nearly 75,000 Sudanese Nubians from the area to be inundated.

The billion-dollar dam, now half constructed, is designed to hold back all the water not immediately required for irrigation. Not a drop is to flow out to sea unused. The added storage capacity will allow Egypt to reclaim a million new acres from the desert and transform another million acres from one-crop-a-year farming to three crops annually. Thus the six million acres now under cultivation will be augmented by nearly one-fourth. This, it is hoped, will enable Egypt to grow the additional food she needs to feed her rising population and perhaps raise the low standard of living.

On part of the new land Egyptian Nubians have already been resettled. About 60,000 of these proud descendants of the one-time rulers of Egypt were moved in 1963 and 1964 from the flood zone south of Aswan to farm villages around Kom Ombo, a sugar-cane-growing district 40 miles north of the dam site.

In Turkey a number of dams were built with foreign aid during the 10-year regime of Premier Adnan Menderes. There has always been controversy about whether the Premier constructed the right dams at the right places on the right rivers. The results have given Turkey hydroelectric power for industries yet to be built, but irrigation gains, which Turkey desperately needs, have been slight.

The Turkish Government now wants to harness the headwaters of the two historic rivers that rise in the mountains of eastern Anatolia—the Tigris and the Euphrates. A power dam, the Keban, on the Euphrates is in Turkey's present five-year plan.

After negotiating for years Turkey obtained help from the United States and other Western powers. The United States held up immediate aid because there were serious questions about the feasibility of the project. There was also an even more serious objection by Iraq to a unilateral decision to use this international river. While the Turks and Iraqis have not been disposed to negotiate on the subject, Iraqis have been somewhat reassured by the statement of the Turks that they are planning a dam for power and not for irrigation that would absorb a large part of the water supply.

In Iran a most ambitious reclamation project to revive Khuzistan got under way in the nineteen-fifties. This province in the southwest corner of the country was once fertile. Some anthropologists believe this area may have been the site of the Garden of Eden.

The Khuzistan experiment in coordinated regional development is frequently called "Iran's T.V.A." for three reasons. First, it is a scheme to develop together all the resources of earth and water to be found in the area. Secondly, it was contracted to the American firm of David E. Lilienthal and the late Gordon R. Clapp, who were among the early administrators of the Tennessee Valley Authority. Thirdly, it is an American-Iranian project.

A spectacularly high dam has been set in the almost perpendicular walls rising from the bed of the Diz River. The surrounding country is as desolate as the moon. A former T.V.A. official employed by the Khuzistan Development Service recalled to me the difficulties and disputes he had encountered in the nineteen-thirties when T.V.A. construction required the resettlement of great numbers of southern families—even whole towns and, "worst of all, several cemeteries."

"Out here," he said joyfully, "there's not a thing living or dead to be flooded."

Diz turbines will feed electric light and power to thousands of Iranians who have never known it. The ambitious plan calls for the development of industry and farms to make use of the power. Some critics say the project is too expensive and too ambitious, but its proponents reply that the same criticism was leveled a generation ago against the T.V.A. itself. Time, they say, will tell.

In comparison with some of the great water sources of the Middle East, the Jordan River is almost tiny. In its final stage, as it meanders toward its resting place, the Dead Sea, it can be passed over almost without notice. But the Jordan River is the center of a bitter controversy today. This is because for part of its course on its western bank lies Israel and on its eastern bank lie the Arab states of Syria and Jordan.

Some of its water flows down from Mount Hermon in southern Lebanon. Some comes from tributaries rising in Syria and some from springs inside Israel. The Hasbani River from Lebanon and the Baniyas out of Syria converge along with the Dan to form the Jordan River at the top of northeastern Israel, about seven miles above Lake Huleh.

Eleven miles below the lake, the river, falling 915 feet, tumbles into the Sea of Galilee, also known as Lake Tiberias. Below this it is joined by the Yarmuk, flowing out of Syria and Jordan, and continues its below-sea-level course to the Dead Sea.

The annual flow of the Jordan is small compared with that of the world's mighty rivers. Its total length is only 200 miles. Moreover, its effectiveness for irrigation purposes is lessened in its lower regions by increasing salinity. It is fed by a number of salt springs in the Sea of Galilee, and that is an important factor in the dispute over Israel's plan to divert water from the upper river.

Small as it is, the Jordan is a resource of great potential to the regions bordering it. And until some practical method of de-salting Mediterranean Sea water is developed, use of Jordan River water is considered vital to Israel. It has been part of Israel's development programs ever since she became a state in 1948.

However, international law gives all countries touched by a river a rightful claim to a share of its water. And Israel and the Arab lands of Lebanon, Syria and Jordan cannot agree on anything. To help bring the opposite sides together on a Jordan River plan, President Eisenhower in 1953 sent out a mission headed by the late Eric Johnston. Mr. Johnston devised a formula for dividing the Jordan waters so that the Arab states would get approximately 60 per cent of the flow and Israel 40 per cent.

Israel accepted the plan, at least in principle. The Arabs did not, and the parties never came to the conference table to discuss it.

The arguments on both sides have been martialed in long tracts. But no amount of persuasion has satisfied the Arabs, whose objections basically are that any joint Arab-Israeli irrigation scheme for the Jordan is an integral part of the whole "Palestine problem" and must be treated within an over-all solution of that problem. To the Arabs this means that joint use of the Jordan must be considered along with the problem of international borders, repatriation of Palestine refugees and many other points of dispute (among which the Israelis would include the lifting of the Arabs' boycott of Israel and the right of Israeli ships to use the Suez Canal). Israel uses the same argument—that of an over-all solution—against demands by the Arabs that she repatriate the Palestine refugees.

However, there is a more fundamental reason for Arab refusal to negotiate a division of the Jordan waters. To do so—to meet at the same conference table with Israeli representatives—would be tantamount to recognizing the existence of Israel. This the Arabs have never consented to do.

Israel now has gone ahead on her own and largely carried out a bold scheme to divert the water she claims was accorded her in the Johnston plan.

On May 5, 1964, Israel announced that she had tapped the Jordan at the upper end of the Sea of Galilee and that water had begun to flow through pipelines to her Negev desert. The announcement evoked a storm of protests from the Arab states, but the threat of war has not materialized. The Arab countries resolved instead at their two "summit" meetings in the United Arab Republic in 1964 to concentrate on their own reclamation plans aimed at using the Jordan's waters for their own purposes.

On their side the Israelis argue that the water is there to be used, and certainly it is needed. The Israelis say they cannot be expected to delay urgently necessary development plans indefinitely because of Arab "intransigence."

The Arabs hold that the Jordan River is "Arab water" because it flows mainly from Arab lands. They argue that, in any event, water crossing national borders cannot be used until all riparian rights have been recognized and resolved. Finally, the Arabs deny that the Israelis are morally justified in taking water out of the Jordan valley to irrigate the Negev, which is in another watershed.

The Israelis say the Arabs deliberately exaggerate the purpose and effect of the diversion scheme. The Cairo press last year accused Israel of "usurping our water" to reclaim the Negev for the settlement of two million more "hostile" Jewish immigrants. But Israeli officials say this would not be possible, that most of the 30 billion to 40 billion gallons of water to be taken each year from the Jordan would be used to replenish sources that are drying up and to take the place of wells now being overpumped. Only a small part of the water, they say, would be made available to open new areas for settlement.

The Arabs, faced with an accomplished fact, will try to go ahead with their own development schemes as fast as they can. It was demonstrated at the Cairo and Alexandria conferences of 1964 that they could not organize a united war, and they decided not to try it.

Developing the Jordan's headwaters in Lebanon and Syria and the Yarmuk River on the Syrian-Jordanian frontier will not be easy. Although the Arabs speak confidently of quick accomplishment, their projects, said to be on the drawing boards, are not moving forward noticeably. Financing is an obstacle. Lebanon, the country that can best afford irrigation projects, has the least need for them, and the Lebanese traders are not too eager to spend money on nonpaying causes no matter how worthy they may be.

It would seem that at least five years will be required for the Arabs to make serious headway, and Israel, with her diversion scheme in operation, has a running start. Meanwhile the worst danger to peace may be expected along the Israeli-Syrian border, which has a long history of shooting incidents. A clash in the fall of 1964, for example, was believed to be directly related to the water issue. It took place in Israel between two springs that feed the Dan River tributary of the Jordan. The Syrians asserted that the Israelis began the fighting that took at least 10 lives to protect those springs, and some diplomatic sources voiced the belief that the Syrians were sensitive about the springs because they were contemplating deep borings to tap their underground sources.

Israeli officials said the Syrians started the attack to "fuzz up" Israel's claim to clear sovereignty over the area and particularly over the springs, whose bubbling waters flow into the Dan and eventually into the Jordan above the point where it is tapped by the Israelis. There have been other incidents since this one and they are likely to continue. Moreover, there will always be a dispute over who was the aggressor and who was the defender.

International opinion will be a key factor in the issue of keeping the peace. The Arabs cannot attack Israel as long as they know the Western powers will quickly intervene on the Israelis' side. They hope this would not happen if they could show clearly that Israel was the aggressor in any spark-throwing incident.

The United States still stands by the Johnston proposal for dividing the waters of the Jordan. Former Premier Khrushchev plainly put the Soviet Union on the Arab side when, addressing the United Arab Republic's National Assembly in May, 1964, he denounced the Israeli diversion plan as "robbing Arabs of their own sources of water."

The Jordan River could lead to war. However, it

might well be the key to armistice and eventual peace in the Middle East. Some new Johnston plan, proposed from outside the United States, might succeed. Certainly new international efforts are overdue.

However, the Middle East needs ever more water. The Jordan supplies insufficient water for its own valley, let alone the Negev desert. Even the Nile, with its vast new Aswan reservoir, cannot long nourish Egypt's growing population.

The only real hope—a cheap way to de-salt sea water on a vast scale—is barely in sight. No energy source yet developed has provided a remedy. Solar energy has been tried without practical result. Both Israel and Egyptian scientists are going their separate ways, experimenting with nuclear energy. They should be working together on the common problem. The United States has already offered help to both sides. It could be the most rewarding project ever carried out in the Middle East.

For access to abundant fresh water would surely relax tensions. With water really to irrigate the Negev in Israel or the Sinai and western deserts in Egypt or the Jordan River's own valley in the Kingdom of Jordan, there would be less interest in animosities along the borders. Gradually there would be less fear of the rising populations across these borders.

XI

Shifts in the Northern Tier

THE ARABS have had no monopoly on Middle Eastern revolutions. In 1960 Turkey overthrew a popularly elected Government with which she had grown dissatisfied. And Iran probably has averted an overthrow because her royal reformer, Shah Mohammed Riza Pahlevi, pressed his social revolution.

The last five years have found both countries of the Middle East's Northern Tier, which adjoins the Soviet Union, in the throes of their democratic growing-up. The term "growing pains" does not adequately describe the ordeal. It has been a labor of Hercules.

In Turkey the legacy of Ataturk was a constitution establishing a republican form of government.

In the 10 years before his death Ataturk, applying dictatorial methods, forged the necessary democratic machinery. The constitution provided for popular government through a combination of the French code and British common law and parliamentary practice. The process of establishing all the trappings of democracy was, of course, not completed when Ataturk died in 1938. Perhaps the most important piece of unfinished business facing Ismet Inonu, Ataturk's successor as President, was providing for an opposition political party. Ataturk had promised one, but never saw fit to permit it to come into being.

President Inonu did see fit, and the Democratic party was established. Its founders were Celal Bayar, who, like Inonu, had been a general in Ataturk's liberation army, and Adnan Menderes, a rising politician from the Menderes River Valley of southwestern Turkey.

In 1950, to the surprise of most politicians including President Inonu, the Democrats in the second election in which they took part won a majority of the Grand National Assembly seats. In the tradition of Western democracies Inonu gracefully handed over the reins of power to the victors. General Bayar became President and selected Menderes to form the Government. Menderes as Premier emerged as the dominant figure and remained Turkey's strongman for 10 years.

Premier Menderes benefited from the first inflow of American aid under the 1947 Truman Doctrine. In the following years he exploited this assistance to the full. As the Marshall Plan restored Western European nations to prosperity, Menderes found he could draw on them too for aid in exchange for guarantees of support against Communist moves in the Mediterranean area. Menderes led Turkey into the North Atlantic Treaty Organization and was, as we have seen, a key figure in establishing what is now the Central Treaty Organization.

His idea of developing Turkey was public works —dams, roads, bridges, factories, schools and mosques. The peasants of Anatolia idolized him. He went out to see them over new roads as he opened new bridges, new power plants, new factories. He was the first Turkish leader to get so close to the peasants, and whenever they had the opportunity —in 1954 and 1957—they voted to retain his party in power. Their enthusiasm for him was heightened by his assuring them good prices for their wheat plus cheap bread, exemption from taxes and new mosques. It is said that during his 10 years of rule Menderes built or restored at least one mosque for each of Turkey's 45,000 villages. The "Menderes minaret" is a landmark throughout the Turkish countryside today.

Educated Turks in western Anatolia and Istanbul were by no means enthralled by the Menderes

performance and became increasingly disenchanted
with it. They accused Menderes of "building Turkey into bankruptcy." They saw the cost of living
rise more than 100 per cent in the nineteen-fifties.
They saw new factories and other industrial facilities fail to produce for lack of raw materials. They
resented particularly the new mosques, the construction of which they regarded as a deviation
from Kemalism—Ataturk's secular statism. They believed the Democratic party Premier was compro-
mising separation of church and state for political
reasons. Finally, Menderes's critics, led by Inonu's
Republican People's party, accused the Premier of
"capitulating" in policy matters to his American
benefactors.

In the spring of 1959 Menderes "miraculously"
escaped injury in a plane crash near London. When
he returned to Turkey, Ankara's Ataturk Boule-
vard was red with the flowing blood of sheep, cows
and camels. The throats of literally hundreds of
beasts had been slit in honor of the leader whose
life "Allah had protected." The sight of the illiterate
Anatolian peasants slaughtering valuable animals,
an old Moslem custom, in Menderes's path disgusted the intellectuals in Ankara and Istanbul.

Menderes was supersensitive to criticism. He responded with repressive measures that most diplomatic observers and not a few foreign correspondents felt to be as unnecessary as they were foolish.

Almost every cartoonist and editorialist with a bent for satire was hailed into the special press court at one time or another, and many spent a few months, perhaps a year, in jail. Political speechmaking was increasingly restricted, and in one instance Inonu, who was then 75, was prevented from addressing a partisan rally.

The last straw was a Menderes decision in the spring of 1960 to ban all political activity—while a (pro-Menderes) parliamentary committee "investigated" political rights under the constitution.

In April university students in Istanbul rioted embarrassingly just as a NATO conference was to convene there. Police and riot squads drove the student mobs back but at the cost of some lives. Then a group of young army officers who had been plotting for six months decided to act. On the night of May 27, 1960, they rolled a few tanks up toward the presidential residence in Cankaya, took over the guard, then moved into the Post and Telegraph Office. In Eskisehir a detachment arrested Menderes as he was leaving a meeting. The Government fell without a half-dozen shots being fired and with hardly any casualties.

The young rebels brought forward General Cemal Gursel, a long-respected army commander on the verge of retirement, to head the revolutionary council, called the National Unity Committee.

More than 500 Menderes Democrats, including

the Premier himself, President Bayar, all members of the Cabinet and all the 425 Democratic party Deputies in the Grand National Assembly, were arrested and held in prison throughout a trial that took nearly a year. In September, 1961, Menderes and two Cabinet ministers were hanged as enemies of the state. Most of the other defendants, including former President Bayar, then 75, were sentenced to prison for terms up to life.

The 17 months of army rule that followed were extraordinary, for the army revolutionaries defied the tradition of entrenching a military dictatorship and set to work preparing for a restoration of reformed civilian government. In October, 1961, a little more than a year and a half after the revolution, Turkey had a new constitution and a newly elected civilian regime.

The constitution provides for a parliamentary government with the bicameral legislature empowered to elect a President for a single seven-year term.

The Turkish elections of October, 1961, held scarcely more than a month after Menderes's execution, showed the political successors of the late Premier to be surprisingly strong. The Inonu Republicans, the old Ataturk party that had opposed Menderes, came out ahead of any of the three new parties that were splinters of the outlawed Democratic party. But no party had a clear majority in

parliament, and the Justice party, a Menderes splin-
ter, pressed the Republicans for actual leadership
in numbers of seats.

The National Assembly agreed on the election
of General Gursel as President but on little else. At
the army's insistence, Gursel appointed Inonu Premier and asked him to form a coalition government.
The coalitions, first with the Justice party and later
with other combinations, came and went. But Inonu
stayed on as Premier for nearly three and one-half
years, redoing much of what he had done as Turkey's leader a generation before, asserting popular
government and reaching for popular rule, political
and economic stability and social progress.

Premier Inonu's Government fell in February,
1965, when the rival Justice party challenged a
budget bill to finance the regime's five-year development program. President Gursel then named as
successor to Inonu not the Justice party leader, as
would have been normal, but a politically neutral
Senator, Suat Hayri Urguplu, who had been a career diplomat holding ambassadorships in Washington and London. The President did this because
he believed the army would not allow a leader of
the party that had inherited Menderes's following
to come to power. The whole point of the revolution, in the army's view, might be lost if the people
it had overthrown were reinstalled by popular
choice.

The first parliamentary election since 1961 was not due until October, 1965. But local elections had brought Justice party victories. The Republicans lost strength, and all the offshoots of the defunct Democratic party moved toward joining the upsurging Justice party.

If the Justice party should win a clear victory in the October election, President Gursel, who still has three years to serve, would be compelled to ask its leader, presently Suleyman Demirel, a member of the Urguplu Cabinet, to form a new government. Would the army let the Justice party leader do it? Or will the army, as in other countries in the Middle East, prove to be the ultimate seat of power?

Sadly, for the moment at least, the bold and brave new Turkey of Ataturk has come to a standstill. In the 40 years since its birth it should have become a lusty youth striking out for the new frontiers of social progress. The will was present, but the way has not yet been found.

The task has been complicated because Ataturk, while directing the Turks to their goal, drove out the foreigners, notably the Greeks, who for centuries had stimulated the business, professional and technological life of the country. The Turks cannot hope to achieve a progressive society overnight or in a generation. But, as President Johnson recently said of Americans, they may not always succeed, but they "are always trying."

* * *

In Turkey's neighbor Iran, much to the surprise of friends and foes and, I am sure, to the irritation of Gamal Abdel Nasser, the Shah has managed to keep his throne since resuming it after the Mossadegh nationalist upheaval.

He has leaned heavily on American help, but more recently his bold program of reforms has made his personal need for underpinning less imperative. Part of the reason, doubtless, is that his aggressive approach to progressive measures has disarmed the post-Mossadegh nationalists and enabled the Government to keep the Tudeh (Communist) party underground and in check.

The Iranians, whom the Shah always speaks of as "my people," were not happy with their monarch's flight to Baghdad and Rome in the face of the Mossadegh crisis. Many thought he should have stayed with them through "hell and burning oil." To them it is still significant that the Shah, a flying enthusiast who is frequently his own pilot, keeps his personal plane fueled and ready for immediate take-off.

The Shah explains his departure in 1953 as one impelled by devotion to his people. It enabled him, he says, to demonstrate that in his absence chaos would reign. This, he declares, added impact to his triumphant return after Mossadegh's fall.

The Shah, who was educated in Switzerland, who

has spent much time in England and France and has visited the United States frequently, is completely Western-oriented. Along with a penchant for tennis, sports-car racing and flying he acquired great fluency in English. He was one of the few English-speaking personages in the Middle East with whom I never felt obliged to avoid colloquialisms and slang. The Shah knew the vernacular well and often used it.

When I asked him about his failure to win the support of prominent Iranian reformers to his own reforms, he replied: "So what? They have their own ambitions."

Flippancy of speech and spirit and a reluctance to acknowledge the contribution of able "subjects" proved shortcomings that the Shah, even in middle age, has found difficult to overcome. Certainly he has lost the support of many wise and good men in business and government who once aided and admired him.

Nonetheless the imperial court in Teheran today offers the interesting spectacle of a Shahinshah (King of Kings) who thinks of himself as a "revolutionary" committed to a revolution at the top for the emancipation of those at the bottom.

New York University's Institute of Fine Arts bestowed on the Shah in June, 1964, an honorary doctorate of laws recognizing his "farsighted vision and personal courage" in forwarding the progress of social reform based on social justice. Nothing could have pleased more the ruler who in 1919 was born the grandson of a poor peasant. The Shah is only a second-generation King of Kings and his inheritance included not only vast feudal estates acquired by his acquisitive father, Riza Shah, but also empathy with peasants and a feeling of their need for a fairer share of the land and its blessings.

Trying to spark reform by his own example, the Shah broke up the vast crown estates—consisting of more than 1,000 villages—in 1950. He tried to persuade, and then to compel, other of Iran's great landlords, numbering about 100, to follow suit. The trouble with trying to legislate land reform was that most of the legislators were landowners and without a real revolution they would remain influential figures in government.

Finally, unable in 1962 to get a serious land-reform bill through the Majlis (parliament), the Shah abolished the legislative body and by royal decree ordered the large landholders to sell their land except for one village apiece. At the same time he instituted a reform Government. This was the beginning of the Shah's "white revolution," an upheaval without coup d'état or monarchial ouster.

Meanwhile there was popular distrust of the government because of a history of fraudulent elections, dishonest and inefficient tax collecting, loose law enforcement and a derelict civil service. So while the "white revolution" began with land distribution, it followed this up quickly with a serious attempt at many administrative reforms encompassing everything from election scandals to traffic violations.

In the absence of a parliament, which the Shah correctly sensed would obstruct his reforms, he submitted the whole program to a national referendum. It received, predictably, an overwhelming "mandate." In addition to land distribution and honest elections, the mandate called for a literacy corps, reforestation projects, the sale of unproductive and unprofitable state factories and other reforms.

Today the "white revolution" is on its way, but it is far from completed and the Shah is still pressing ahead. The land distribution is in a second phase— to reduce further the maximum land one man may own. This is difficult in Iran because, unlike Egypt where all arable land is basically much the same, Iranian land varies in quality. On fertile soil along the Caspian Sea a family can prosper on a few acres, but in the dry central and southern plains a family's livelihood may depend on control of 200 to 400 acres.

The Shah's literacy corps, drawn from high-school graduates in military service, has been a bright spot of his revolution. An army of 10,000 Iranian youths has taught 400,000 village children to read and write. Now the corps is being expanded to include graduates of schools of medicine, dentistry, veterinary science and pharmacology. Carrying the educational drive a step further, a "development corps" is taking on a variety of tasks in agricultural extension work and general village improvement.

This last undertaking is of utmost importance. For while making peasants the owners of the land they farm is the foundation of land reform, its value is determined largely by the ability of the new peasant landholders to work together in cooperatives.

These cooperatives must take over the functions of the former landlords in buying and selling, irrigation and drainage, often in providing credit and loans. Education, certainly the elementary ability to read and write, is a requisite of cooperative operation. The peasants must make the cooperatives work, and about 80 per cent of the more than 20 million Iranians are still illiterate.

The Shah's fear of the Soviet Union has abated recently. While he has a mutual defense pact with the United States, he has promised Moscow not to allow Iran to be used for foreign bases. Neither the United States nor any other power has bases in Iran, but in 1950 Washington began providing the Shah with military supplies and training assistance on a large scale.

In 1963 the merciless Communist propaganda attack on the Shah ceased, and he has since shown progressively less interest in spearheading Western defenses against Communist aggression. While he previously insisted that the headquarters of the Central Treaty Organization be moved to its geographical center in Teheran, he now seems content to let them remain in Ankara. The Shah has also given up his urgent requests that the alliance have a unified military command with full United States participation, just as NATO has.

If the Shah today is less alarmed about the Soviet Union, he is increasingly restive about the United Arab Republic. Iran's monarch and Nasser, though pursuing many common objectives in their respective countries, are archenemies. Friction, beginning when the Shah took Iran into the Central Treaty Organization, led to a break in diplomatic relations between Cairo and Teheran when in 1960 the Shah showed signs of extending full recognition to Israel. A *de facto* relationship between Iran and Israel has long existed, and a commercial agreement provides for the shipment of Iranian oil to Israel's port of Elath. Also the Shah uses Israeli experts for technical assistance. However, the Shah has never established diplomatic relations with Israel and so there is even yet no exchange of envoys.

The Shah and Nasser keep up a running fire of mutual denunciation. The Shah suspects every

Arab unity move as a threat to him. The present alliance between the United Arab Republic and Iraq
could bring Nasser to the Shah's borders, a prospect
that distresses him.

The Shah is also disturbed by evidence of Nasser
strength in oil-rich Kuwait, Iran's neighbor at the
head of the Persian Gulf, and in the Arab sheikdoms nearby. The Shah believes Nasser is aiming at
control of the oil resources of the gulf, which, to
the Shah's added irritation, Nasser insists on calling
the "Arabian Gulf." The United Arab Republic's
leader does little to assuage the Iranian monarch's
fears.

After seeing all the evidence of struggle—the
stubborn Turkish devotion to Ataturk's revolutionary ideals and the later "white revolution" in Iran—
one wonders about the future.

Aside from Western-oriented Israel, Turkey has
probably done more than any other Middle Eastern
country to replace dynastic rule with popular government. It achieved one peaceful orderly transfer
of power when the Inonu Republicans bowed
gracefully to the Menderes Democrats in 1950. It
suffered relapses later, and finally the Army left the
barracks to replace Menderes in 1960. Now, after
four years, the restored civilian government is not
functioning well and there is danger of new intervention by the army.

The Shah has foresightedly bolstered his position. But he has only made the beginnings of establishing orderly procedure to guarantee free and honest elections. If he were incapacitated tomorrow, the "white revolution" would be in grave danger of changing to a more violent color.

The Arab countries, with perhaps the exception of Lebanon, have no popular governments worthy of the name. Republics are born by coup d'état and fall as quickly, the people having little to do with either the birth or the death. Even the oldest and most staid of them, Nasser's United Arab Republic, is, as a shrewd observer has noted, "neither united, nor Arab, nor a republic."

Even so, the yeast of popular government is in ferment in the Middle East. This is apparent in the various struggles. The future may not be clear, but the currents of change suggest directions. We shall consider them in the last chapter.

XII

Currents of Change

At the beginning of this book we noted that the Middle East enjoyed relative unity under the Ottoman Empire—and slept through it. We noted too that the strife, the turmoil, the boiling-pot atmosphere of the Middle East in the 20th century had roots deep in political intrigue in which foreign powers looking after selfish interests were often involved.

There remains to be shown the positive and perhaps the most far-reaching result of this unheaval. The foreigners brought social impetus as well as political intrigue into the area. One way or another this has penetrated every corner of the Middle East since World War I.

Ancient sleepy villages have seen modern armies

march past. In the First World War, Allenby's British troops moved up through the Holy Land from Egypt. In the second great war of this century the British and Hitler's Germans fought with tanks and land mines across the Libyan desert almost to Alexandria. United States lend-lease supplies to the Soviet Union were transported over newly laid blacktop roads from the Persian Gulf to the Caspian Sea.

These villages today know the roar of jet planes overhead. And on the roads donkeys and camels grudgingly move aside for automobiles and diesel-powered trucks. In Teheran I have seen a London-style double-decker bus yield the right of way to a sheep herder maneuvering his flock to market.

Evidences of foreign aid are apparent everywhere—tractors (often misused as family conveyances), electric water pumps, steel plows (all too few), experimental poultry farms, hybrid seeds.

With the introduction of the transistor radio and television, illiterate backward people have begun to hear, see and even comprehend the outside world. They get a glimpse of advances made by ordinary men in other countries.

The impact of television in Egypt and Iran, where TV systems have been in operation for some years, is enormous. When I wrote about this once a high-school reader in New York challenged my statement that boys and girls in Cairo had developed a craze for cowboy suits as a result of looking at American Western movies on the new Egyptian television.

"How can families earning less than $150 a year afford television sets?" my critic asked.

Actually $150 is a figure close to the average individual income and many Egyptian families earn more than that. But the point is that in a controlled society such as Egypt's it is not necessary to have a TV set in every home for television to be effective. The Government, which oversees the distribution of available sets, makes sure there is at least one in every village—in the community center if there is one or in the open square or in front of a central coffeehouse. The villagers flock around to see the most exciting entertainment in town.

And villagers all over the Middle East can afford transistor radios. I saw them even in Yemen, where they were almost as common as the status-symbol rifles and daggers. Walking through Taiz and Sana, I saw small Japanese sets, imported from the free port of Aden, slung over the barrels of shouldered guns. I remember being startled once to hear the BBC news blaring from a Yemeni tribesman's radio. But usually the proud possessors of transistor sets had them tuned to a broadcast they could more readily understand—Cairo's "Voice of the Arabs."

The cotton field hand in the Nile Delta and the Yemeni tribesmen learned of President Kennedy's assassination only a few minutes after people in the streets of Washington, London or Paris. I heard the news along with 1,500 Sudanese attending a basketball game in Khartoum. It was shortly after 9 P.M. when the tragic report, received over someone's radio, began circulating around the open-air court. Because of the difference in time between the Sudan and Texas it was in fact less than an hour after the shocking event in Dallas had occurred. Within 15 minutes Sudanese began paying calls at the homes of American families living in Khartoum to express their sorrow and sympathy. I learned later that similar visits were being paid at the same time in every capital of the Middle East. President Kennedy in his relatively short tenure had captured the friendship of the Middle East as had no other President of the United States—and so far President Johnson has not been able to approach this. But the rapid arrival of the terrible news through radios in remote backward towns and villages added special dramatic impact for the peoples living there.

The Middle East, of course, adheres to the law of nature that every progressive push may expect a backward pull. I would list at least four pulls that continue to hold the Middle East back.

1. *Religious Traditions.*   The Shah of Iran has told intimates that his most formidable opposition was not the reactionary landlords but the ultraconservative *mullahs* (religious leaders). They have

rebelled stubbornly against land distribution and reform, arguing that it is against Koranic teaching to take a man's property from him against his will. Actually the Moslem organization everywhere, including Iran, owns vast lands which it exploits for its own gains. The Iranian *mullahs* dispute the Shah's right to take from them "Allah's lands." The Shah insists, however, that he, not the *mullahs*, is Allah's principal representative in Iran and that his voice speaks Allah's will today.

Before taking over the religious properties in Egypt in 1961, Nasser, moving slowly and with great tact, obtained a favorable ruling from the important sheiks. They have announced a finding of no conflict at all between Nasser's Arab Socialism, including land reform, and Islamic teaching.

Moslem tradition is to act only if "God wills" some deed to be done. *"Insha 'allah* [God willing], I will see you tomorrow," our Egyptian cook invariably said on taking his leave each night. If he were ever so bold as to assert that he would be on hand next day without interjecting an *"Insha 'allah,"* God might well smite him during the night. In practice God is often put on the side of inertia, for if a man on rising in the morning feels indisposed he is entitled to draw the conclusion that God wills his sickness and he had better stay home.

There is in the Moslem tradition, too, a straight-laced morality that when carried to extremes works against social and cultural progress. The fact that President Nasser makes Egypt's famed "belly" dancers cover their midriffs before stepping on a stage is probably unimportant, except as an indication of Moslem "hard shell" moral attitudes. It is something else again, however, when even in modern times young men and women in much of the Moslem Middle East cannot mix socially save in the presence of members of their families.

However, in the Middle East, religious ultra-conservatism is not a problem for Moslems only. There is an open fight in Israel between secularism and Jewish orthodoxy. Conservative rabbis want the Zionist state to adhere strictly to ancient law and practice. They are demanding an absolute observance of the Saturday sabbath. They are insisting that hotels, restaurants, planes and transatlantic steamers prepare and serve only kosher food. The secularists argue that some of these practices are not suited to modern needs. Government and business, not to mention weekend tripping, cannot come to a dead stop over Saturday. And confining public eating places to kosher cooking is defeating the Government's program to promote tourism.

2. *Age-Old Habits.*   Peasants everywhere resist new methods of farming. The *fellaheen* of Egypt want to use the same broad-bladed hoe that their ancestors used in Pharaonic times. They employ this implement to break up the soil for planting or

for digging the little ditches that guide canal water through their fields. The tool has served well and the Egyptian peasant is expert at using it. But technical advisers try to point out how modern plows and cultivators could increase crop yields.

The Land Reform Ministry in Egypt has a difficult time persuading families to move onto newly reclaimed farm lands, even though it will mean higher incomes. The Nubians of Upper Egypt consented to migrate 100 to 200 miles north into what they regarded as "foreign country" only because they would be flooded by the Aswan High Dam's waters if they didn't. Even so, the Egyptian Government in transferring them *en masse* had to take great pains to move whole villages intact and to keep each resettled village in its old Nile line-up. Neighbors insisted on retaining neighbors, and adjoining villages had to continue to adjoin in their new location.

3. *Bureaucracy.* Revolutionary governments from the Nile to the Euphrates and beyond still operate with the old overcrowded, irresponsible, indifferent civil service inherited from the Ottoman Empire. Plans for streamlining, whether in Nasser's Cairo, the Shah's Teheran or post-Ataturk Ankara, get tangled and choked in administrative red tape.

Even in Nasser's new nationalized factories the old habits are perpetuated. The workers are Government employes who find that showing too much

initiative may prove a mark against them. In some
instances—of course, not all—the old habits of
overemployment and underproduction have low-
ered the efficiency of the factories taken over "in
the interests of the people." The new factory bosses
vigorously assert that their workers now have real
incentives to work harder and produce more than
ever because of higher wages and profit-sharing.
But many who have traveled about the Middle East
in recent years wonder whether Nasser may not
soon find out, as have the Turks and the Iranians,
that nationalized factories can become white ele-
phants living on instead of contributing to the
economy. Indeed, the Russians themselves, we
now hear, are experimenting with "private capital
enterprise."

4. *Poor Health.*   Every Middle Eastern country
boasts of its new schools, its new clinics, its socialized medicine. But virtually all have serious and
sometimes crippling health problems resulting from
bad sanitation, ignorance and malnutrition. In
overcrowded Egypt forward strides have been made
against trachoma, the eye disease. But the debilitating bilharzia, which attacks the intestines, has yet to
be coped with. This parasite, which spends one cy-
cle of its life in the snails that inhabit the canal waters and another in the human beings that drink,
bathe or wash clothes in those waters, is not an immediate killer. It saps the body of strength and,

like the semitropical climate, enervates the victims. Unfortunately the disease is widespread throughout the Nile Delta region.

On balance there is a net gain. Certainly there is the restlessness, the awakening that is usually the harbinger of progress. But it is doubtful if the peoples—Arabs and non-Arabs, Moslems, Christians and Jews—are ready for meaningful unity. And peace will be much longer coming.

If Nasser or some other leader not yet in sight could by some magic deport all "imperialist" influence and leave the Middle East to its own devices, there would still be a long touch-and-go transition. For the new governments and regimes want time to test their wings. They are not ready to settle for someone else's panacea—even Nasser's Arab socialism. They are in the stage of muscle-flexing and development but hardly of cohesion. This stage is well known to all Western democracies. Certainly it should be to the United States, where one war was fought to make possible the creation of a union and another much more bitter one to preserve it.

In fact, foreign influence will not and cannot leave the Middle East. Acting against such a development are many factors: the international character of the state of Israel; the European and American interests in controlling Middle East oil; Communist aspirations to form the minds of the rising educated generations of Middle Easterners; the de-pendence of present and probably future regimes on foreign economic and military aid; and, finally, the determination of Gamal Abdel Nasser, the advocate of nonalignment, to align Arabs, Asians and Africans against "imperialism and colonialism."

Education and cultural exchange stimulated by foreign aid will breed enlightenment in the Middle East. It will be the significant development of the generation just being born. It will not bring the end of turmoil in this turbulent region right away—it may at first even spark new restlessness and even revolution.

However, I feel that the next generation, flowering 25 years from now, will make it extremely hard for governments to change hands overnight by a coup d'état of a few insiders. By the year 2000 a majority in the Middle East may be healthy enough and schooled enough to insist that the leaders share with their people some responsibilities of government. This would lead to popular revolutions of the kind experienced in England, France and the United States in the 18th and 19th centuries.

This, however, can happen only if the West maintains contact with the Middle East. Despite all Nasser may say about Arabs going it alone, the average young Egyptian or Iraqi or Iranian or Turk today wants to be like a Westerner, preferably an American.

"It would be a lot more fun if the Americans were here instead of the Russians," a young Egyptian engineer told me at Aswan.

The young Arab, wherever he is, wants to wear Western clothes. He loves American soft drinks and frozen chicken, and regularly attends American movies. He wants to speak English and studies hard in off hours. He wants to attend a European or American university, although a year or two in the United States is financially out of reach for any Arab without government help. Let no reader be mistaken about this. The young Middle Easterner aspiring to a career looks to the West whether or not he agrees with all our policies.

There must be Communist sympathizers among the young people, but I never encountered a young man or woman who aspired to go to a university in the Soviet Union. Soviet scholarships, offered aplenty, go begging in Cairo today. We should encourage this Westward look by continuing all forms of contact—foreign aid, student and teacher exchanges and trade.

Fundamentally United States policy in the nineteen-sixties is to support Israel and promote the stability that will protect the vast American oil interests in the Arabian peninsula and Iran. The welfare of the Arabs and their aspirations for independence and unity (if they are compatible) is of secondary importance. There is no secret about this. The Arabs have been informed by both word and deed, and they have accepted the policy, knowing that it is to their interest to keep the petroleum flowing out of the ground and moving to the markets of Europe. The chief function of the Suez Canal today is to expedite both the flow of oil and the returning profits.

It is not necessary, I feel, for the United States to change its policy in order to get along with the Arabs or to keep them out of the clutches of Communism. The Communists, as I have pointed out, have their troubles. It is not necessary to love the Arabs, although a little more understanding of them and their predicament would help carry out our policy.

Supporting Israel while keeping the Arab pipelines (and the Suez Canal) open is an act requiring the calm, patience and daring skill of a high-wire performer. Moreover, we must take care that everything happens in the open.

The secret agreement in 1960 between President Eisenhower and Chancellor Adenauer of West Germany to give Israel $80 million worth of American-made arms set off an Egyptian–West German–Israeli embroglio in 1965. Nasser reacted violently when he finally learned about it. Yet when President Kennedy advised Nasser in advance that the United States would supply Israel with Hawk missiles, there was no outcry and no "crisis."

President Kennedy took pains to keep all the Arab leaders informed of United States plans in the Middle East. By doing so he won their confidence without giving them a thing. In an interview with *The New York Times,* Nasser said he "admired" General de Gaulle of France because "he is frank."

"I would rather deal with him than with one of his diplomats," said Nasser, who disagrees with de Gaulle on many points, "because he means what he says."

Patience is required, particularly when President Nasser tells his people, as he did at Port Said, that the United States can stop its aid and "go jump in the lake." Greater patience is required when Egyptian authorities permit an African "liberation" mob to burn down the United States Information Service library. Nasser's discourtesy is aggravating to those who know that American wheat is feeding the *fellaheen* listening to him and that the same wheat enables him to boast that he is raising the people's standard of living. It is frustrating for an American to see in ruins a library that had the best technical reference shelves in Cairo, and one wonders about the reaction of the hundreds of Cairo university students who used it every week.

However, the Senators who demanded an abrupt cut-off of aid to Nasser were wrong, and the State Department was right in appealing for continued aid to Egypt in these circumstances. Arab tempers are short and our purposes long. Regardless of Nasser's discourtesies, it is paramount that young Egyptians and Arabs everywhere keep looking toward the West. I feel it requires at the least our keeping in touch with them.

The bedouin in the Arabian desert, the peasant of Anatolia and the Jordan River Valley, even the nomad in mountainous Iran are finding out that the modern world is big and that there is much in it that is new under the sun. These people are expecting more from their land and their leaders than did their ancestors. Profound changes will inevitably come. Nasser would have a far more difficult time satisfying his people with a one-party government a quarter century from now. If the changes are for the good, the Western foreigner, Nasser's "imperialist," may take his share of the credit, just as he must take much of the blame if things go wrong and strife and ferment persist.

The same patience and skill are required on the Israeli side. As I have said, I do not think the Israeli and the Arabs will become good neighbors in the time of the present rulers. They all participated in the hostilities. But time will remove these veterans from the scene, and their successors will focus their telescopes not so much on the frontiers of Israel as on the great region before and beyond.

One of Jordan's chief exports is Palestinian

brains—exiles and sons of exiles are now advisers to Government ministers in Libya. There are engineers and architects in Saudi Arabia, doctors in Pakistan. Money they send back is a main source of Jordan's revenue. Palestinians are regarded, generally, as the ablest of the Arabs, and probably those who have had opportunities for advancement would not be content to go back to the basically unviable strip of land Israel occupies.

Similarly, young Israelis are growing up who do not understand fully their parents' attachment to the Jewish homeland. Their brains too are being exported—on technical aid programs in developing Africa, for instance. Their indifference may in time match that of young Arab Palestinians.

Broader perspectives, a broader outlook, broader opportunities may lead a future generation to a land and a life that are really promising.

INDEX